SECRET VOICES

FROM

THE FOREST

Thoughts and Dreams of
North American Trees

VOLUME TWO: THE MIDCONTINENT

Text and
Illustrations by

Laura J. Merrill

Myth & Magic
Taos, NM

Published by: Myth & Magic
           PO Box 612
           Taos, NM 87571
           laurajmerrilltreetalker.com

ISBN-13 978-0-9848299-2-7

Library of Congress Control Number: 2014912340

All poems by permission, © Brian R. Mitchell
All artwork © Laura J. Merrill
Artwork photographed by Andrew Neighbour
Cover/interior design by Mary Neighbour and Laura J. Merrill
Edited by Jénnet Grover

Printed in the USA

First Edition

10 09 08 07 06 05 04 03 02 01

CONTENTS

CHAPTER ONE: The Great Plains

CHAPTER TWO: The Great Lakes

< iii >

< Volume II >

CHAPTER THREE: The Upper Midwest

CHAPTER FOUR: The Lower Midwest

< v >

< Volume II >

CHAPTER ONE

THE GREAT PLAINS

spirit herds still run
freely under the wide sky;
their wind bends the grass

>>>>>>>>>>><<<<<<<<<<<

THE GREAT PLAINS

The Earth's landmasses have separated, then joined, separated again and rejoined, several times over the many millions of years of its history. At the core of most modern continents is a *craton* (from the Greek, *kratos*, meaning "strength"), formed of igneous and metamorphic rock that melded, under great pressure, when the Earth surface was more volatile. At the center of the North American continent is the Laurentian craton, and like other interior regions of tectonic plates of the world, this formation is deep, stable, and solid.

The North American Interior Plains were born over this ancient rock bed, when other continents slowly collided from the west and east, forming mountains that prevented water from flowing freely to the oceans.

Around a hundred million years ago, most of the Interior Plains were covered by an enormous, shallow sea, which divided the continent in half. It contained everything from microscopic organisms, plankton, mollusks and algae, to massive sea reptiles and thirty-foot-long sharks. When the landmass, always moving, eventually lifted, the sea dried up, leaving vast amounts of sediment. To this was added sediment eroded by runoff from the mountains on either side. The resulting sedimentary rock, relatively flat terrain, and the soil created by wind and water — in the form of rain, flooding rivers and the advance and retreat of glaciers — is what lies underneath these great grasslands.

The Interior Plains extend from the Appalachian to the Rocky Mountains, and from the Arctic nearly to Mexico. The westernmost portion is known as "the Prairie" in Canada, and "the Great Plains" in the United States. Not simply flat and featureless, the plains are home to mountains, once-active volcanoes, sand dunes, caves, *badlands* (heavily eroded regions with little vegetation), plateaus, steep *escarpments* (high cliffs resulting from movement along geologic faults), and extensive *loess* deposits (fertile wind-blown silt).

Rivers, great and small, have been significant forces in shaping the land of the plains, and continue to be a source of erosion, despite extensive damming.

Because most moisture coming in from the Pacific Ocean is released on the western slopes of the Rockies, the amount of yearly rainfall in the interior of the continent can be significantly lower than elsewhere, averaging only twelve to twenty inches in many places, although conditions become more humid from west to east.

Lack of precipitation is not the only thing that creates challenging growing conditions for plant life. Winds (coming from the west, the polar regions, and the Gulf of Mexico) create highly fluctuating air masses that can allow temperature ranges to differ fifty degrees or more within a single day; persistent drought can extend from a year to several decades;

‹ 2 ›

‹ Secret Voices from the Forest - Volume II ›

herds of animals can overgraze, and frequent fires can destroy too much. However, occasional fires can be beneficial, since the prairies are greatly composed of underground roots, which remain, keeping the grasslands intact.

Although by no means completely treeless, the principle flora is grass of different species, heights and composition, and other flowering plants. Technically, grass *is* a flowering plant; in this context, the other plants are usually called *forbs*.

Grasses are one of the most recent developments in terrestrial plant evolution, appearing about forty million years ago. They were one of the groups that evolved to survive increasingly dry conditions and lowering levels of carbon dioxide in the atmosphere. With smaller leaf surfaces and other water-conservation mechanisms that decrease the rate of evaporation, grasses absorb sunlight during the day, but conserve energy by photosynthesizing at night. They also form extensive fibrous root systems, which connect one plant to another, forming a dense mat, up to twelve feet deep in some places, and three or four more times in volume than what appears above ground.

Grasslands and herbivores seem to be made for each other, and though we picture herbivores to be bison, antelope, and cattle, others consume a much greater percentage of plant matter. These are prairie dogs and other rodents, ants, and soil microorganisms (numbering in the billions, *per teaspoon*), bacteria, protozoa, fungi, algae, *nematodes* (microscopic roundworms), and mites. Nematodes, feeding on roots and smaller multi-cellular life forms, consume more plant matter in a given acreage than any group of animals living in the same area above ground.

< 3 >

Many animals made the plains their home before the glaciers retreated. The largest land animal in North America today is the bison, but once there were lions and cheetahs, mastodons and woolly mammoths, camels and llamas, saber-toothed cats and giant beavers (at eight feet long), horses, giant tortoises and even a nine-foot-long saber-tooth salmon. It is believed that these creatures disappeared primarily because of the changing climate. Today, the animals may be smaller in stature, but all play an important role in this disappearing ecosystem.

< The Great Plains >

REFLECTIONS ON DIGNITY

What Elm Can Tell You About Itself

I stand in a perpetual attitude of one who waits to embrace the bounties of Nature. I exemplify *Dignity* by passing my allotted time in peace, accepting circumstances that cannot be changed; but, more than that, I face — *with joy* — each event as it unfolds. The wind blows as it will, and with it comes rain or drought, and thereby an extension of my time here or a lessening of it. Each particular phenomenon contains a world of experiences unto itself.

I see dignity all around me: in those whose time in this world is short — in the Mayfly, who has a single day to will its species to continuation before it dies; in the sickly infant, who has not the strength to endure, and yet inspires love; and in the mountains, whose understanding of time and motion is so far removed from those of us who surround them as to seem to be of another world.

I was once a toad. This was an adventure, and I found it interesting to move about, and to be so small that I was easily propelled by outside forces. Of course, in my current form, I am often transformed — made into objects by man. It allows for a sense of perpetuity, although one's vision becomes somewhat skewed in the process.

So now it is important that I maintain a sense of myself as an individual — standing alone, even when there are others present. To teach this, by example, is another way of ensuring the future. In dreams, I am following the path my roots take underground. Although I am blind, there is an urgency to move forward. I am finding small treasures hidden in the walls of the caves we are forming in our progress — little gems, little creatures, little worlds unto themselves, where one may become something different than before.

Here on the prairie I can see the curve of the Earth, and the enormity of the sky. I give shelter to birds that travel a long distance. My ancestors taught me that protection of the young and the weak, whether one's own, or those of others, will secure one's place in the future. In turn, I hope to pass on that endurance is often a matter of chance, but it does not mean that the effort should not be made.

Elm's Place in the World

My species knows that energy can be directed through thought alone. Will has a strong impact, but is more eruptive, and a less accurate means. We elms see all things in geometric forms, which fit into each other like puzzle pieces, and are especially partial to triangles and cones. We have also observed that everything has gotten smaller over the many thousands of years we have existed. It is as though the world is being compressed into ever-tightening forms.

We speak to other trees of rhythm. It is in the movement of leaves and branches in the wind; the rise of sap in the spring; the pulse of the air in the heat of summer. All these things are part of the pulse of the seasons. Movement and time are the same. As you go forward in time, you are moving, even if you are standing still.

We believe that there is such a thing as death, because we see lives end all around us; but the energy that was once contained in one organism or form has to go somewhere, so perhaps death is a kind of passageway after all. Desire is what moves us out of a static state of existence into a variety of forms, both in this life and in others. Acceptance of circumstances does not mean giving up. Like lightning, we are here to create an entranceway for the power of cosmic energy to enter the density of the earth, to recharge the surface of the planet.

Elm's Message to Us

You all seem very busy, although it appears that this stems from emotional requirements. As such, you are more a force than a group of individuals, led by urges that originate in the makeup of your bodies. This is no different from the collective energies of other species, as all are driven to survive. The more of you there are in number, the more powerful the force of your intent.

< 6 >

Your time may teach you to question, to challenge yourselves, as you are another reflection of the whole. Ask what, how, and especially *why*. If you do, you will waste less time on melodramatic, reactionary extremes.

Creativity should always be encouraged, though profit and productivity are constantly at war with the creative urge, testing it to gauge its purity. Conscious appreciation of the gifts of the Muses can elevate the consciousness of mankind out of the commonality of survival.

There are countless opportunities to behave with dignity in the face of opposition or tragedy, because that is when this quality naturally manifests. Those are the times when you have the greatest chance to evolve, the times when you can choose how you respond to the things you cannot control, or circumstances you cannot change. Listen to your inner voice. Those who *become* Dignity are also those who change the course of events and create Magic.

< Secret Voices from the Forest - Volume II >

CHRONICLES

< 7 >

Ulmus americana is a deciduous tree native to middle and eastern North America. In ideal conditions, it is fast growing, and can reach heights of 100 feet or more, with a massive trunk seven feet in diameter. While it is, by nature, a forest tree, it often stands alone, and takes root easily along fence lines and roadsides.

Like seventy-two per cent of all flowering plants, the American elm has "perfect" flowers, with both male and female parts. Although each tree's flowers contain both sexes in a process called *dichogamy*, one sex's parts develop before the other. In the elm, the female parts develop first, and then, when they are receptive, the male parts develop and produce pollen. However, though the American elm is hermaphroditic and capable of self-pollination, it usually cross-fertilizes with the pollen from another elm via wind-dispersal. Its seeds have tiny wings that can carry them on the wind for a quarter-mile, or help them float down streams or rivers.

< The Great Plains: American Elm >

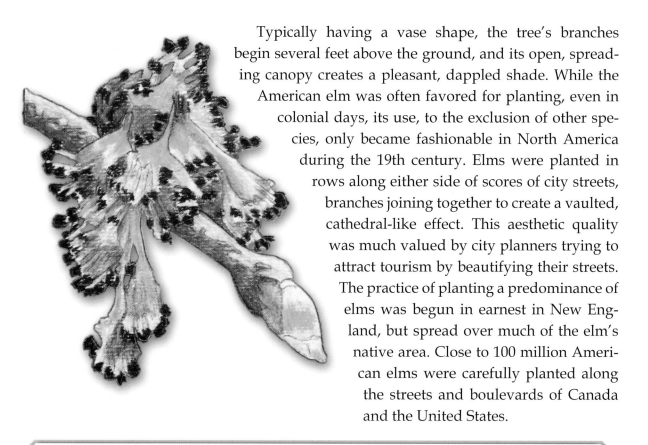

Typically having a vase shape, the tree's branches begin several feet above the ground, and its open, spreading canopy creates a pleasant, dappled shade. While the American elm was often favored for planting, even in colonial days, its use, to the exclusion of other species, only became fashionable in North America during the 19th century. Elms were planted in rows along either side of scores of city streets, branches joining together to create a vaulted, cathedral-like effect. This aesthetic quality was much valued by city planners trying to attract tourism by beautifying their streets. The practice of planting a predominance of elms was begun in earnest in New England, but spread over much of the elm's native area. Close to 100 million American elms were carefully planted along the streets and boulevards of Canada and the United States.

The boulevard itself has an interesting history. The word "boulevard" has its origins in the Dutch word *bolwerc*, later becoming *bulwark*, which was the term used for the flat part of the ramparts, or embankments, used for the defense of a city or castle. For a great part of its history, Europe was plagued by wars between royal houses seeking wealth and property, but there were also times of peace, and in 1668, a particularly significant treaty gave Louis XIV of France the confidence to demolish the outer walls of Paris, replacing them with wide, tree-lined streets. These were not heavily used until the 19th century, when members of the burgeoning bourgeois class began taking drives in their well-appointed carriages to parade their new wealth for the benefit of their neighbors.

Between 1852 and 1870, under Napoleon III, Paris went through a period of urban modernization that made extensive use of a network of boulevards, avenues and open spaces. Although they were primarily constructed to provide ease in moving troops about the city to squelch uprisings, these improvements and "greenings" were of great benefit in that they, along with sewers and other public facilities, improved social and sanitary conditions for the common populace. Trees in the city were becoming a commonplace sight.

Around 1930, a shipment of wood arrived in the United States, containing the eggs of bark beetles which carried a fungal disease known as Dutch elm disease, or DED, not because of where it originated, but because of where it was identified—the fungus itself originated in Asia. DED interferes with water transport, thereby stopping nutrients from circulating in the tree, which slowly kills it. The pathogen spread rapidly, exacerbated by a lack of understanding of the potential problem and a particularly violent 1938 New England hurricane, where the highest concentration of elm plantings were located. The hurricane left many thousands of downed trees in its wake, providing the perfect breeding ground for the bark beetle, which carried the fungus. The final blow came when the United States entered World War II, and funds could no longer be directed at fighting the spread of the disease. In the end, 77 million elms were dead, and the disease still affects elms today.

After the war, the pesticide DDT was used to combat Dutch elm disease, and the trees were heavily sprayed, which had devastating effects on populations of robins and many other birds. Observation of this sad outcome was one of many things that prompted Rachel Carson to write *Silent Spring*, published in 1962, warning of the dangers of the indiscriminate use of chemical pesticides to the health of humans and nature alike. Her book was instrumental in the eventual banning of the use of DDT, and is widely credited with inspiring the modern environmental movement.

Some experiments in cloning were attempted, but the American elm, always thought to have twice the usual number of strands of DNA, was difficult to cross with other species of elm. There have also been several *cultivars* developed—plants that have been selected for breeding—both in Canada and the U.S., which show promise as having an elevated resistance to DED.

But the most promising research has come about through the discovery that about 21% of elm trees in the wild have *two* strands of DNA, rather than the supposed *four*. These elms, still thought to be of the same species, are naturally resistant to the fungus, giving hope that the species will recover naturally over time.

In a survey taken to find out what tree was the most favored in North American history, the elm got number one status, with twice as many plantings as the nearest competitor, the Live oak.

ELM COMPANIONS

Prairie Climbing Rose
Slender Walker Snail
Orange Spotted Sunfish
Bladdernut
Yellow Morel
Western Chorus Frog
Evening Primrose
Monarch
Broadleaf Wood Oats
American Bison
Orange Butterfly Bush
Poison Ivy
Whooping Crane
Northern Grasshopper Mouse
Baldwin's Ironweed
Field Cricket
Duck Potato
Horned Lark

we all liked to go
and stand near the wide trunk
looking up at the branches cantilevered out
like galleries and stairs with all those rooms
for housing life   even in winter with the life
packed away beneath bark
as though to a meeting house
for wind and rain   or in spring again
at the hanging out of new leaves that will later
calm the hot sun   everyone knew if you went there
to be with it in the one land you didn't go
   proud   we all remember
      that tree   the big elm
         the great house

FACTS ABOUT SOME AMERICAN ELM COMPANIONS

American bison

The term "buffalo" originated in the 17th century with French fur trappers, who called the bison *boeufs*. Though altered in translation, the name stuck.

Bison were instrumental in establishing North America's first primitive roads. When their great herds migrated between seasonal feeding grounds, they instinctively avoided low-lying areas, which could be treacherous with mud or deep snow drifts. Their paths, or "traces," were followed by the Indians, and later by white explorers and pioneers. While most were oriented north—south, several of the trails going east—west were used as a template by the railroads.

The American bison's coat is almost always dark brown, but once in a very great while a calf is born white. This rare animal is considered sacred by many American Indian tribes, and its birth is a significant spiritual event.

< 12 >

Joseph Chasing Horse, traditional leader of the Lakota Nation, tells the story of the White Buffalo Calf Woman, who appeared 2000 years ago, during a time of famine. She brought The People a sacred bundle in the form of a pipe, which is kept to this day on the Cheyenne Indian reservation in South Dakota. At that time she taught them songs and dances, along with seven ceremonies: purification (or the sweat lodge), child naming, healing, adoption (or the making of relatives), marriage, the vision quest, and the Sundance (which was for all the nations). The sign that the time of her return was near would be the birth of a white buffalo calf. Then she would purify the world, bringing back harmony and spiritual balance.

Duck potato

Sagittaria latifolia is a reference to the constellation Sagittarius, whose astrological symbol is an arrow, describing the shape of the leaf of this perennial aquatic plant.

Colonies are widespread throughout the continent. Tender tubers, protruding from their roots, are consumed not only by many animals, but were a staple food for many American Indian tribes, who prepared them in the same way as potatoes: boiled, dried, roasted, mashed, ground into flour, or candied with maple sugar.

< Secret Voices from the Forest - Volume II >

Field cricket

Male crickets attract mates by chirping, a sound produced by rubbing modified veins on their wings across each other. These structures act much like a comb and file, one wing having a scraper and the other having a series of wrinkles. The frequency of the chirping varies. It is believed that one can estimate the outside temperature by counting the number of chirps in 15 seconds and adding 37.

Males clear a small platform in front of their burrows from which they broadcast their song. A female hears it through her *tympana*, or eardrums, located just below the bend of her front legs, and crawls to the burrow, as she cannot fly. Once she reaches him, he will move back and forth in a courtship dance.

Poison ivy

More than 350,000 people are affected by poison ivy annually in the U.S.A. It is good to know that if the plant is burned and the smoke inhaled, a rash could appear on the inside of the lungs that is painful and sometimes fatal; if eaten, it can adversely affect the mouth and digestive tract.

In the category of "when Nature creates an ill, she also creates the remedy," a study published in 1958 showed that applying a preparation of Jewelweed relieved most patients poison ivy symptoms within two or three days.

On the other hand, an extract of the leaves of poison ivy is used extensively by homeopaths for rheumatism, ringworm and other skin disorders.

< 13 >

Whooping Crane

Standing nearly five feet, the Whooping Crane is the tallest North American bird, yet it only weighs around fifteen pounds. Both males and females perform elaborate dances to attract mates, running, leaping, bobbing their heads, flapping their wings, and calling loudly.

Once found throughout the Midwest, with an estimated population of around 10,000, by 1967 their numbers had diminished to only twenty individuals, and they were declared endangered. A co-operative conservation

< The Great Plains: American Elm >

effort between Canada and the United States has since brought the total number of birds to about 600.

A successful way of reestablishing migration routes is used by members of an organization called "Operation Migration." They rear young Whooping Cranes in isolation and train them to follow ultra-light aircraft. Bill Lishman and Joe Duff pioneered this method in 1993, when they led Canada Geese from Ontario, Canada, to Virginia and South Carolina. After the success of their efforts, the U.S. Fish and Wildlife service asked them to spearhead the work being done with Whooping Cranes. Their goal is to establish a self-sustaining migratory flock by 2015.

Prairie Climbing Rose

This rose is North America's only native climbing rose.

In ancient times, the image of the five-petal rose was omnipresent, and in nearly all cultures, sacred to the mother goddess. The apple, also in the Rose family, with five pips arranged in a star formation, was venerated as a feminine symbol. The number five itself has great significance, and each of these symbols has found its way into many religious structures, as a hidden acknowledgement of the sacred feminine.

< 14 >

Northern Grasshopper Mouse

About the size of a small hamster, the carnivorous *Onychomys leucogaster* is a nocturnal hunter of beetles, grasshoppers, spiders, and scorpions, as well as birds, other rodents, and even snakes. It makes loud, high-pitched howls or whistles right before attacking prey, marking territory, or mating. Its predatory behavior and strong social bonds with mates and offspring sometimes elicits comparison to coyotes and wolves.

Yellow Morel

Morels, highly prized among mushroom-hunters and chefs for their flavor, are perhaps the best known of edible fungi, as they have a distinctive appearance.

Recent studies by the U.S.D.A. have shown that the morel is able to

< Secret Voices from the Forest - Volume II >

inhibit the negative side effects that grapefruit compounds have been shown to have on some pharmaceutical drugs.

Slender Walker Snail

Mollusks are a large group, estimated at 200,000 species, containing such members as clams, oysters, squid and octopuses. From this group, only snails and slugs are terrestrial.

There have been several mass extinctions in the planet's history. The largest of which, beginning around 250 million years ago, eliminated possibly 95 per cent of all species. Studies support the theory that this particular episode was slow and gradual, triggered by warming ocean temperatures and the slowing of oceanic currents, which produced low levels of oxygen in the water. Additionally, there was a high level of volcanic activity, and conditions for life became too adverse. As a consequence, mollusks, better able to survive such circumstances, became the dominant life form at that time on Earth.

Evening Primrose

Evening primrose, named for its habit of blooming after sunset, can be any of over 140 species of wildflower native to most of North America. The species illustrated here is *Oenothera biennia*, whose bright yellow blossoms open rapidly, in under a minute, and only last till noon the next day. They contain a nectar guide, visible to us only under ultraviolet light, that helps pollinators locate it.

Oenothera biennia is the source of evening primrose oil, widely used as an anti-inflammatory and as a treatment for a variety of minor skin conditions. The human body requires but cannot produce an omega-6 essential fatty acid called *gamma linolenic acid*. There are only a few foods that contain this nutrient—evening primrose, borage, and black currant seeds. Although claims are made regarding its value in treating a wide variety of serious illnesses, little conclusive evidence exists, due to poorly executed studies.

⋞ BOXELDER ⋟

REFLECTIONS ON THE FALLOW EARTH

What Boxelder Can Tell You About Itself

There is a dimension where the essential spirit resides, in which all possibilities exist, in which the illusion of opposites does not dominate the mind. This region is present at all times. Once the knowledge of this realm has been attained, it may be revisited simply by the desire to do so. As it was said, "The Kingdom of Heaven is spread upon the Earth. . . ." The *Fallow Earth* is always exactly what it is, and has always been — the only thing that is dormant is the comprehension of this truth.

Because I know this, I can be wild and free, growing as I please, with spontaneity. I am always blessed with what I need, and am content and fruitful anywhere, but I admit that Spring, the time of exuberance, is the time I feel most at one with the moving force of creation. At that time I know what it is to be God.

I am able to, and do, make my home in a variety of areas, but particularly prefer the Plains. However, though we like the open spaces, individuals of my species often elect to seed themselves in a neighborhood with other kinds of trees, because we like company, and because we are less likely to be disturbed in a crowd. We trees tend to jostle for space, particularly in urban areas, so you can hear mutterings of, "Gimme some room!" if you listen carefully. Living near people can be precarious, as their behavior is unpredictable and they like their chemicals, but there are many advantages, if you are noticed and appreciated.

More than anything, I want to know the "how" and the "why." For that reason, it is important that I be understanding of others' situations. Protection means something different for everyone. When I was a porcupine, I used to make myself bigger by having sharp spines that stuck out and hurt anyone who might attack me. Now I find that I can protect others. At other times, while still being myself, I was no longer growing and green, but I found that even though my own active life was over, I could still provide shelter for others. Understanding teaches compassion.

You may think it odd, but sometimes I dream of falling, of no sense of "me." I just move through space. It is very freeing to have no form. It is how the birds must feel.

Boxelder's Place in the World

My family, the Maples, likes to celebrate life. Seriousness is unnecessary melodrama about things that cannot be changed. Being unhappy never solves a problem.

< 17 >

< The Great Plains: Boxelder >

Members of my own species are the counselors; everyone else expresses to us. Trees feel stress, too! Though we know all is as it is meant to be, we still experience changes that disturb us, that pose threats, like everything else. Since the early times, when we became who we are, the atmosphere of the Earth has become more confusing, or perhaps it is just crowded. Whatever the reason is for this situation, more concentration is now needed to completely focus. Boxelder's aim is to aid in the attainment of tranquility, in the ability to live to the fullest extent, without fear, and that requires focus.

My species has learned that the tiniest ones, the microscopic things, are watching closely. Their capacities and contributions are mostly misunderstood or overlooked. We may realize this because the Boxelder is the "least" of the Maples, and "like understands like."

Boxelder's Message for Us

There is no such thing as "lack," but it is sometimes necessary to comb your area to find what you require. However, knowing that you will find it, without effort, is the secret of the Fallow Earth.

You are Wind-talkers. This makes you move things from place to place more quickly than they might be able to migrate on their own, so you speed up or change evolution. It remains to be seen if the effects of this contribution effects are negative or positive. You, like all others, have the need to self-protect, but you also have the capacity to see beyond the fear of your own deaths, to a true understanding of the permanence of matter. You could use this ability to slow down a bit, and enjoy yourselves.

You would be wise to pause in your busy endeavors to reflect on the present state of affairs, focusing on the planet as a whole. Working the earth with your hands can be a way to make contact, although it is easy to get sidetracked when you set short-term goals that cause you to enter into a "battle with Nature." No plant is a "weed;" no animal is a "pest."

Practice your innate gift of forbearance. Nature is not an enemy, and if you allow yourself to listen to her many voices — which are calling quite loudly to you at the moment — then you can make appropriate changes without effort, as there is no effort in caring for friends.

< 18 >

< Secret Voices from the Forest - Volume II >

CHRONICLES

The Boxelder, also known as Boxelder maple, or Maple ash, is a native species of maple that has several regional name variants which refer to its similarity to other trees: its whitish wood is like that of boxwood, and its leaves are like some species of elder and ash. It is the only North American maple with compound leaves, which can resemble poison ivy.

The Boxelder, at a maximum of eighty feet, does not reach exceptional heights, nor, at an average of seventy-five years, does it live to a great age, but it is the most widely distributed native maple on this continent and, perhaps because it quickly colonizes disturbed areas, such as abandoned fields, roadsides and open ground in cities, it continues to spread outside its natural range, even to western China and Australia.

‹ The Great Plains: Boxelder ›

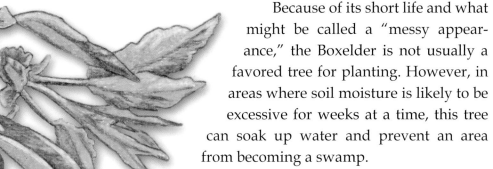

Because of its short life and what might be called a "messy appearance," the Boxelder is not usually a favored tree for planting. However, in areas where soil moisture is likely to be excessive for weeks at a time, this tree can soak up water and prevent an area from becoming a swamp.

This is a *dioecious* species, which means that some trees have only flowers with male parts, while other trees have flowers with only female parts. Although stumps and damaged stems re-sprout vigorously, creating multiple-stemmed trunks, both male and female trees are needed to reproduce over the long term. The fruits, typical to the Maple family, are A-shaped, winged keys called "samaras." They can be an important winter food source for birds and other animals, as they often remain on the tree until the following spring.

Sap is plentifully produced, and can be used to make syrup, although it does not make a product as sweet as sap from the Sugar maple. The sap also contains a considerable amount of *mucilage*, a thick, glue-like substance that helps the plant store food and water, as well as a *demulcent* medium which, because it coats the throat and soothes irritated tissues, is sometimes used as an ingredient in cough mixtures.

Boxelder seed pods, which are found only on the female boxelder tree, are favored by the Boxelder bug, a half-inch long, red and black bug that can be noticed in great numbers in fall. They do not bite or cause extensive damage to any plants. Although these insects can become an annoyance to property owners, the use of insecticides is not recommended, as it does not reduce their population numbers in the slightest. The best management scheme, should they enter your home, is considered to be a broom and dustpan.

In 1959, species *Acer negundo* was identified as the type of wood used by the Ancestral Pueblo Indians to make the earliest known wooden flutes of the Americas. A number of these flutes, remarkably still in perfect condition, were found during a 1931 archaeological excavation located in present-day northeastern Arizona.

Carbon-dated to between 620-670 AD, these flutes were fashioned as a rim-blown, open tube, with six holes that created tones ranging over one and a half octaves. They were approximately twenty-nine inches long and about an inch in diameter, and were decorated with red, blue and black feathers from various colorful birds. Pueblo flutes are still made today by members of the Hopi and Jemez Pueblos, who, along with several other tribes, are descendants of the people of the Ancient Pueblos.

The Ancestral Pueblo homeland centers on the Colorado Plateau, covering some 130,000 square miles in Utah, Colorado, New Mexico, and Arizona. The area averages 5,000 feet above sea level and is very dry. Pueblo cultures began to emerge around 2,300 years ago, renowned for building stone and adobe brick structures that housed planned communities for many hundreds of people. Remains of some of these dwellings can be seen at Chaco Canyon, Mesa Verde, the Aztec Ruins, Bandelier, Hovenweep and Canyon de Chelly National Monuments and Parks. The Taos Pueblo, built around the same time, and continuously occupied for over a thousand years, is today a National Historic Landmark.

Formerly referred to as "the Anasazi," a Navajo term meaning, "ancient enemy," the Ancient Puebloans are well known for their beautiful pottery, carved pictures and symbols on rock walls—thought to have great astronomical and religious significance—and great, wide roads extending many miles, seen today in satellite imagery from space.

Around the 12th and 13th centuries, they began to migrate away from these great structures. The reasons for this are probably many, but the most likely, and most straightforward explanation is climate change, in the form of a 300-year drought that began around 1150 CE. Tradition holds that the Ancient Puebloans had achieved great spiritual power and control over natural forces which they used to cause changes never meant to occur. It is believed that the significant effort made to dismantle religious structures at Chaco was meant to make amends to Nature for a perceived abuse of power.

However, at that time, as today, water was the defining issue. Many believe that the Ancient Puebloans simply moved to locations where access to water was more secure. Today, most of their descendants live along two great western rivers, the Colorado and the Rio Grande, with diverse lifestyles, languages and social structures.

< 21 >

< The Great Plains: Boxelder >

BOXELDER COMPANIONS

Ornate Box Turtle
Carolina Anemone
American Bittersweet
Black-tailed Prairie Dog
Boxelder Bug
Spreading Dogbane
Cooper's Hawk
Barnyard Grass
Shovelnosed Sturgeon
Wild Gooseberry
Bullsnake
Red-eyed Verio
Polyporus Squamosus
Common Sunflower
Black-footed Ferret
Bur Oak
Milbert's Tortoiseshell
Purple Top

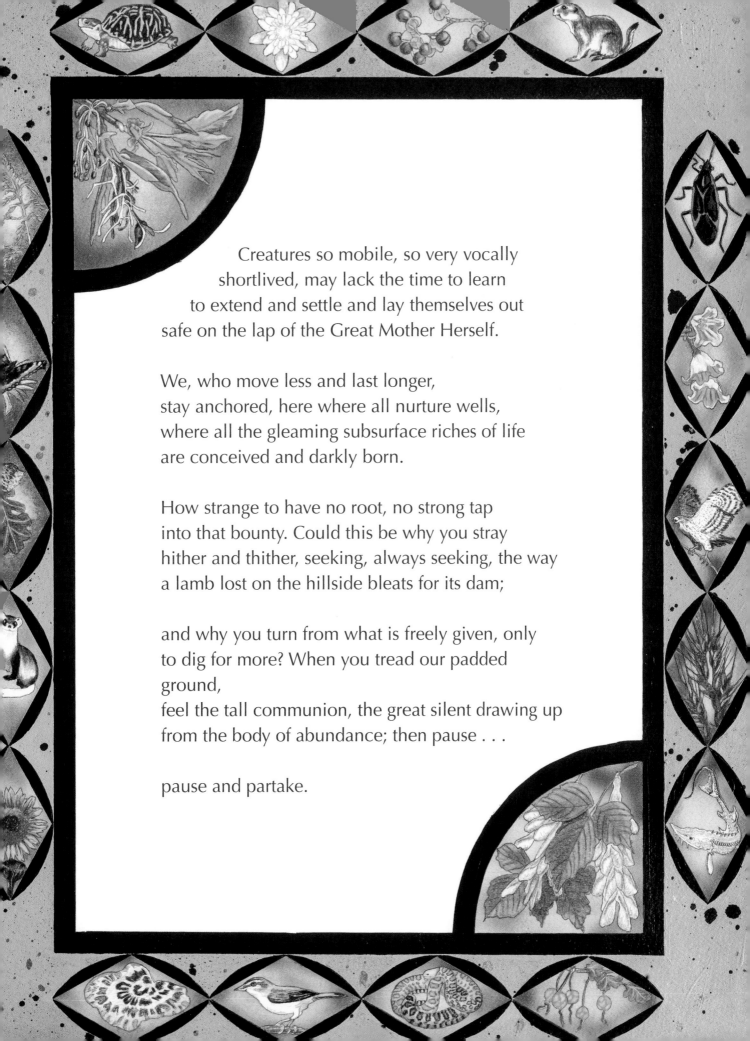

Creatures so mobile, so very vocally
shortlived, may lack the time to learn
to extend and settle and lay themselves out
safe on the lap of the Great Mother Herself.

We, who move less and last longer,
stay anchored, here where all nurture wells,
where all the gleaming subsurface riches of life
are conceived and darkly born.

How strange to have no root, no strong tap
into that bounty. Could this be why you stray
hither and thither, seeking, always seeking, the way
a lamb lost on the hillside bleats for its dam;

and why you turn from what is freely given, only
to dig for more? When you tread our padded
ground,
feel the tall communion, the great silent drawing up
from the body of abundance; then pause . . .

pause and partake.

FACTS ABOUT SOME BOXELDER COMPANIONS

Bur Oak

The Bur oak is a massive, slow-growing tree, with the largest acorns of any North American oak. It is an important food for wildlife, but the tree only produces a large crop of nuts every two or three years, in an evolutionary strategy called "masting." *Mæst* was an old English word that referred to the meat of nut bearing forest trees. So many nuts are produced at once that they cannot all be eaten; so some survive to become seedlings.

Fire was common on the prairie, as well as drought and poor or rocky soils. The Bur oak is tolerant of all these conditions, and is often found standing alone, or in open savannas, where grasses are actually the dominant members of the plant community.

Many cultures saw the oak tree as a symbol of strength and supernatural powers, attributing these to the sky gods. Some American Indian tribes thought it was bad luck to claim victory in advance, and originated the tradition of "knocking on wood" to ward off the ill effects of bragging.

Black-footed ferret

Black-footed ferrets are native to North America, unlike ferrets found in pet stores. They are solitary animals that depend on Prairie dogs for over ninety per cent of their diet, and live in Prairie dog burrows.

Like many species who suffered near-extinction when the prairie was turned into farmland, the Black-footed ferret is the subject of intensive co-operative efforts by private individuals and charities, state and federal government agencies, and Indian tribes, who are working to save the species and reintroduce it into its natural environment.

Boxelder bug

We like to call all insects "bugs," but the familiar red and black Boxelder bug, amongst about 80,000 *other* species, is a *true* bug. True bugs have piercing and sucking mouthparts, which work like a straw, and they have hard wing covers that only cover half the wing, called *hemielytra*.

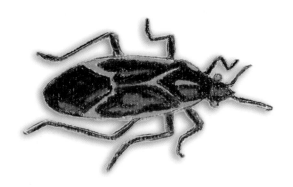

The Boxelder bug feeds almost exclusively on seeds from various species of Acer, or Maple, and from female Boxelder trees in particular, as they bear the seeds. Because Boxelder bugs secrete a bad tasting chemical compound that deters predators, they are able to congregate in very large numbers near their host plant, which is when they are usually most noticeable. They are not known to bite or cause property damage.

Polyporus squamosus

Also known as Dryad's saddle and Pheasant's back, *Polyporus squamosus* is a common fungus found in spring, sticking out in a shelf-like formation from the lower portion of dead tree trunks. One can grow to two feet across, and though edible, is not considered a delicacy, although its fibers have been used to make a stiff art paper. This is a species that is important to forest ecosystems as a decomposer of wood, sometimes taking hundreds of years to recycle the nutrients from a single tree.

Ornate box turtle

Called "ornate" because of the elaborate yellow, brown, and orange-colored pattern of its shell, this land-dwelling turtle of the Great Plains may spend its entire life within an area of only two or three acres. The Mississippi River is usually the furthest east it ranges, preferring open spaces to woodlands.

A box turtle's breastplate, or *plastron*, unlike other turtles, is hinged, allowing it to draw all its body parts completely inside its shell, which protects it from predators.

A baby box turtle is about the size of a quarter. Studies have shown that there are twice as many females as males, which is due to the temperature at which eggs incubate. Temperatures over 83 degrees will produce 100% females.

Wild gooseberry

There are over eighty species of gooseberries and currants native to North America, and most can be eaten. Here are two favorite old recipes:

Syrup: Crush two cups of berries, and combine with 1/2 c. honey and 1/2 c. water. Boil until the liquid is a syrupy consistency.

Pie: Combine four cups berries, 1/2 c. honey and 4 tablespoons of flour, place inside a pastry crust, dot with butter, add a top crust and bake for 45 minutes at 350 degrees. It's yummy.

Black-tailed Prairie dog

< 26 >

The prairie dog, a stout ground squirrel, is only found in the dry grasslands of North America, where it is considered a "keystone species," because its large series of burrows creates a habitat that benefits many other animals and plants. One such is the Black-footed ferret, who depends upon the Black-tailed prairie dog for food, and its burrows for shelter. Black-tailed prairie dog colonies can range in size. As few as five make up a "coterie," consisting of one male and his harem of one to four females, and their immediate offspring; but prairie dog "towns" can reach immense size. One of these in Texas was reported to cover 25,000 square miles and include 400 million individuals.

Prairie dogs greet each other by touching noses or turning their heads sideways and touching incisors. They also groom each other, and burrow construction is a communal effort.

They use their wide range of calls—yips, growls, barks, wheezes, chirps and chattering—to communicate with each other. If there is danger, one prairie dog begins the warning, which spreads throughout the colony. When the threat has passed, one prairie dog will leap in the air and yip an all-clear call, and soon the whole town will be yipping and jumping.

Sunflower

Our native Sunflower was domesticated and cultivated by indigenous Americans,

< Secret Voices from the Forest - Volume II >

possibly as long as five thousand years ago, when seeds were selected for the best size and shape to produce the largest crop. They were used to make flour, cooking oil, dye, and medicinal ointments. It has been suggested that the sunflower was domesticated before the maize plant. Some American Indian tribes planted sunflowers as a "fourth sister" to the combination of corn, beans, and squash.

Early Spanish explorers took seeds back to Europe around 1500. In 1716, the English granted a patent for a process of squeezing oil from sunflower seed. By 1769, sunflower oil had become a popular commodity with members of the Russian Ortho-dox Church, because it was one of the few oils not forbidden during Lent.

By 1830, the manufacture of sunflower oil had become a commercial enterprise, and Russian farmers were growing over two million acres of the plant. By 1880, sunflower seeds called the "Mammoth Russian" were being marketed in catalogs in the U.S.

Canada began the first government sponsored breeding program in 1930, and because of high demand for sunflower oil, production grew. More recently, because of increasing concerns about high cholesterol in the diet, demand increased further, and U.S. production took off. Today the sunflower is the most important native crop plant produced in the United States.

< 27 >

Red-eyed Verio

The Red-eyed Verio is a common summer resident of broadleaf forests whose singing is legendary. It tirelessly repeats short individual phrases, as many as forty to sixty per minute, and holds the record for most songs sung in a single day—22,197.

This migrant breeds in North America, but when fall arrives it begins the long trip to Central and South America, where it will overwinter. In the Southern Hemi-sphere, its diet consists mainly of berries and other fruit. However, in North America, the customary fare is insects. The Red-eyed Verio moves slowly through the treetops, foraging for caterpillars, gypsy moths, fall webworms, tree hoppers, scale insects and aphids. Because it is so successful in controlling these insects, it is considered a crucial protector of forest health, and its declining numbers are of concern.

< The Great Plains: Boxelder >

⪼ AMERICAN PLUM ⪻

REFLECTIONS ON UNTAMED

What Plum Can Tell You About Itself

When you think of the fruit of a plum, you will picture in your mind a small orchard tree, well-behaved and laden with large, juicy purple fruits, sweet to eat; but this idealized specimen has been grafted, pruned and hybridized, and is no longer aware of its own will. I am no one's creation; I am unfettered, free to do as my nature dictates. I go where I please, and resist outside forces. I am *Untamed*. By following my own nature and inclinations, I am able to comprehend the true nature of my form, and the particulars of its processes — seed to sprout, then to tree and flower and fruit, and then back to seed.

This is the essence of nature itself. Of course, there is pattern and design — otherwise form itself would not exist. And within each form are other patterns, each organized by function, and the functions unite to create units, and those units join to create something larger — and so it goes on out into the universe. But in order for this process to be dynamic, there must be resistance. There must be an element that is uncontrollable, an element that is untamed. Otherwise, all would be predictable, static, and unlikely to evolve.

Those who preceded me learned that it is wise to be noticed, to possess something that is desired and required, but not so much as to inspire the insanity of greed, whereby one may be completely consumed. My gift to the future, in turn, is the knowledge that beauty has the power to excite and motivate, even to transform and purify the character of the observer.

I love living on the Plains. There is a sense of quiet enchantment that is always present, that underlies everything. It is as if there is a great subterranean beast, so large that we cannot see where it begins or where it ends, and all those who live within and around it receive nourishment from its beating heart. We work tirelessly to give connection and function, from the smallest microbes to the waving grasses to the grazing animals, the wind and the rain.

I was part of a curtain of rain once. This was a brief incarnation, but it was instructive. Weather is the active part of Earth's atmospheric system, and I, as a tiny drop of rain, was a member of this endless cycle. At the same time, I came to comprehend the artistic qualities of Nature, in that rain can be a thing of stirring beauty.

Plum's Place in the World

The one thing you can be sure of is change. Sometimes it comes about quickly and violently, as a tornado, and sometimes it occurs gradually, eroding the earth with a gentler, steadier wind. In either case, it is a certainty. My species has had to learn to adapt to varying conditions in order to survive, and sometimes there are those of us who are unable to do so. In conversations with other trees, they, too, speak of constancy and change, closeness and emptiness, the twisting of root and branch into earth and sky, and what new objects and creatures they touch in the dark and in the light.

My family, the Rose Family, is all about attraction, about creating a world in which sensation is king. I, myself, am a pinpoint of bright elegance in a place where colors are painted in broad strokes. My species' place in the world is to provide feast in the face of privation to those who would find me beautiful, in comparison to the artifice of an imitation, secondary, and lifeless creation.

You might think it odd, but we dream of space-travel, although not in ships that go from place to place. Rather, I refer to the universe between "here" and "there" that one may traverse in the mind. The wheeling of a large flock of birds leaves traces in the air that are visible for a brief time after they have passed on. Those traces are a clue to the movement of another, sister galaxy.

Plum's Message to Us

< 30 >

You have the ability to conquer death. You do it by breaking through the veil of time, but it happens in your mind. For now, you are concentrating on rapid communication through machines; but the mind itself can work even more quickly. You have the innate ability to discern the emotions and raw thought forms of all others, not just humans. But this ability has been largely abandoned for verbal and written language—not "sacrificed," because the ability is merely dormant. It is possible to learn to unite the two processes, if you learn to believe in what you would call instinct. It would also be necessary to be unafraid of having one's outer image, if false, stripped, and of having dark secrets revealed.

It is part of the basic nature of humanity to follow, to fit in. However, leaders always emerge. What the leaders' inner urges and qualities will be is also dictated by the nature of the time and events. Opposition leaders arise, who will also be a product of the times. Then there will be the rare ones that, like distant stars, move according to a sense of inner gravity, and are in tune with a great vision. Those few are *untamed*, in relation to the rest of the species, and will lead you forward.

< Secret Voices from the Forest - Volume II >

CHRONICLES

Prunus americana is a species of wild plum native to the eastern two-thirds of Canada and the United States. Although an individual trunk can reach heights of twenty feet under ideal conditions, the plant normally grows as a large shrub, whose root system extends indefinitely by sending out *propagative suckers*, or sprouts. Eventually forming a dense, thorny thicket, it not only gives habitat and cover for many birds and small animals, but it is effective in controlling erosion along the banks of a stream or river. American plum only lives about twenty years, but because it clones, a plum thicket can remain long after the original plant dies.

< 31 >

The American plum thrives best in full sun. As part of a forest system, it will either be a *pioneer* species, existing on the edges of the forest, or if the taller, mature trees of other species allow in a great deal of light, it will become part of the understory.

Succession is a series of changes in the variety and structure of species of plants and animals within an ecological community. Although there are many variables — the type of soil, amount of moisture, elevation, effects of animals on vegetation, and so on— succession can be seen as a more or less predictable process by which a few pioneering plants and animals enter an area that is barren, for one reason or another, establishing a community that becomes increasingly complex until it reaches a self-perpetuating stage known as a *climax community*, such as we see in an old growth forest. The American plum, as a pioneer species, may not be part of the climax community.

In early to mid-spring, the American plum is covered in sweet, white blossoms, which will transform into bright red and orange fruits. They have been used to make tasty jams, jellies and wine for as long as there have been humans present to do so.

Before the sugar that we now take for granted was available as a sweetening agent, there was honey, and sap from maple trees, which Indians tapped and collected; but until

< The Great Plains: Plum >

European settlers brought iron pots to America, they were unable to produce sugar crystals from the sap. The maple syrup and sugar that could then be produced was highly valued by Native tribes, and from then on was used in making and preserving many traditional foods.

Indian nations all over the land had many different uses for the plum, other than food: the roots made a dye, the bark, cough medicine and a disinfectant wash; twigs tied in bundles became brooms; crotched sticks were used as dowsing rods to locate underground water; the blossoms were observed to be a seasonal indicator of when to plant corn, beans and squash; dried plums could be turned into game pieces; and young sprouts were made into wands which were used to invite members of other camps to observe the Sun Dance ceremony. Guests came as supporters of a particular "candidate" who wished to secure supernatural power or aid for himself or for his community.

< 32 >

< Secret Voices from the Forest - Volume II >

The Sun Dance ceremony was usually held near the time of the Summer Solstice, and lasted from four to eight days, depending on the specific nation's practice. Common ritual elements included dancing, singing and drumming, experiencing of visions, fasting, and, in some customs, self-torture. The Shaman was the sole authority, and the only one who understood the mythologies and true significance of each part of the ceremony.

This was the most important religious ceremony of the 19th century Plains Indians. The American bison, the primary food animal for these peoples, was a central figure—it was of vital importance to the tribe's survival that the pact between this sacred animal and the People be honored once a year, celebrating a renewal of the cycle of life, death and rebirth.

In some stories, it was the Buffalo itself that gave the ceremony to the People. A buffalo skull might be used as an altar, as it was believed that the soul dwells in the bones of people and animals. Using skeletal remains in a ritual signified a mystical rebirth into the primeval womb, in preparation for a return to life in a fleshy form.

The Sun Dance ritual symbolized appeasement to the buffalo for having to be killed and eaten. It was believed that the buffalo willingly offered itself to the People as food, literally, as a sacrifice of the god. In return, it was felt appropriate to offer sacrifice in return, in the form of fasting, thirst and self-inflicted pain. These actions were considered a prayer for the welfare of the participant's family and community.

< 33 >

Family members and friends came to pray and support the dancers, as well as members of other camps, who were invited to attend through the presentation of an invitation wand, made from the sprout from a plum tree, "about as large as the largest quill from an eagle's wing, and four spans long. Its smaller end should be ornamented with a design of such color and material as the maker may see fit, though all [wands] for one event should be so nearly alike that there should be little choice among any of them, so as to give no cause for a thought of discrimination in the invitation." Those who successfully completed the Sun Dance in its fullest form established that they possessed the four great virtues: bravery, generosity, fortitude, and integrity, and were henceforth respected and honored by all the people. It was expected that each would soon receive a vision, in which there will be a communication from the Sun.

< The Great Plains: Plum >

AMERICAN PLUM COMPANIONS

Pasque Flower
Grey Myotis
Wild Turkey
Green Ash
Mycena leaiana
Juniper Hairstreak
Mexican Hat
Prairie Racerunner
Tape-leaf Flat Sedge
Walleye Pike
Dandelion
Cocklebur
Pictured Grasshopper
Piping Plover
Coneflower
Squashvine Borer Moth
Alkali Sacaton
Swift Fox

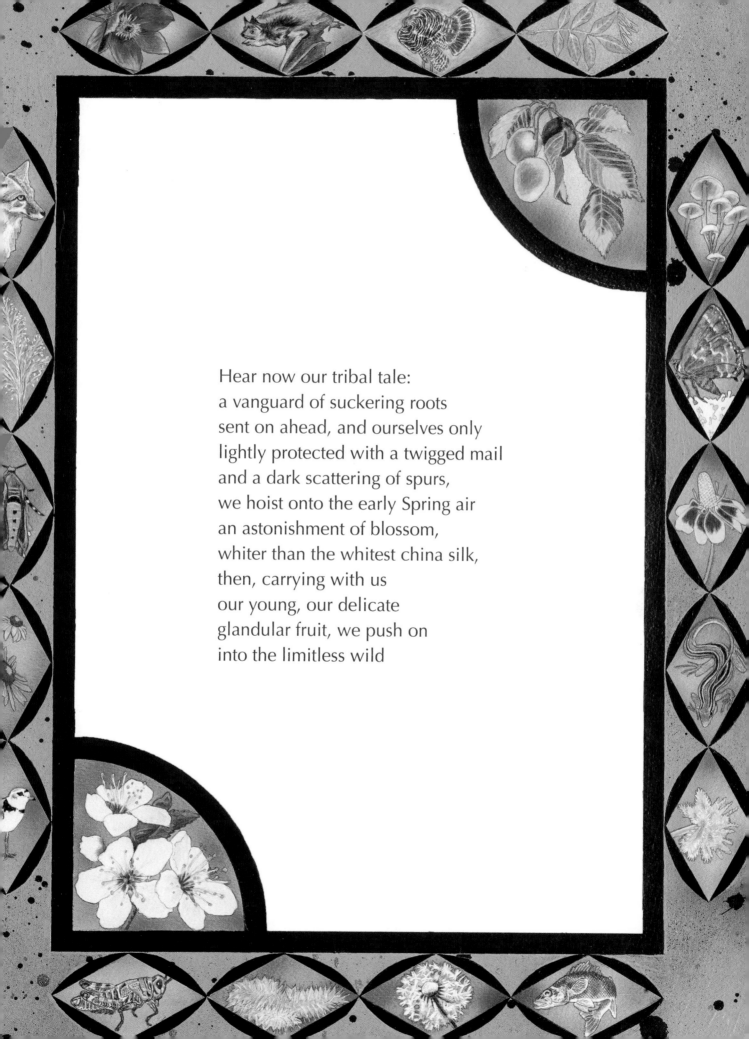

Hear now our tribal tale:
a vanguard of suckering roots
sent on ahead, and ourselves only
lightly protected with a twigged mail
and a dark scattering of spurs,
we hoist onto the early Spring air
an astonishment of blossom,
whiter than the whitest china silk,
then, carrying with us
our young, our delicate
glandular fruit, we push on
into the limitless wild

FACTS ABOUT SOME AMERICAN PLUM COMPANIONS

Pictured grasshopper

Grasshoppers are disliked in agricultural societies all over the world because of the occasional huge swarms of them that wipe out farmers' crops. In the folklore of North American Indian tribes that relied on growing crops, grasshoppers were often portrayed as greedy, careless, or untrustworthy, and were thought to bring bad luck and disharmony. In the Hopi tribe, children who disobeyed elders or violated taboos were told that the grasshoppers would bite off their noses.

On the other hand, tribes who were primarily hunter-gatherers had little issue with grasshoppers, so in their traditional stories, grasshoppers were the good guys, predicting the weather and bringing rain.

Dandelion

< 36 >

The Latin name for the Common dandelion is *Taraxacum officinale*. It not only has a time-honored history as a medicine and general tonic, the name *officinalis*, from *officina*, meaning a workshop or pharmacy, is a reference to its value as a medicinal herb, and it has been so used by the Chinese, American Indians, Europeans and Britons, and was even mentioned in the writings of Arabian physicians in the tenth and eleventh centuries.

It has been, and still is, widely used as food—as a raw or cooked vegetable, as wine, tea, and as a coffee substitute.

Dandelion flowers open as soon as the sun appears, and close again at dusk or when there is heavy cloud cover.

The familiar, bright yellow flower contains a large amount of nectar, and is important to beekeepers. Dandelion's successive blossoms provide bees with a steady supply of pollen and nectar from early spring till late autumn.

Swift fox

At five to six pounds, the Swift fox is the size of a small domestic cat. It hunts and moves primarily at night, and is called "swift" because it can run at speeds up to thirty miles per hour. A very sociable animal, the Swift fox is not particularly territorial, and uses many different burrows, but nevertheless, mates for life.

< Secret Voices from the Forest - Volume II >

The Swift fox, like the American bison and the Black-footed ferret, was an integral part of the prairie ecosystem. The little canine has suffered near-extinction because of loss of habitat and shortsighted policies, but in the last three decades, a number of Indian tribes, charitable organizations, and state and federal agencies have been working together on several reintroduction projects. With some good, though slow, results, there are high hopes for a stable population in the future.

Pasque flower

The common name of this flower refers to Easter, as the flowers are usually in bloom in early spring, but its "first bloom" was the subject of Plains Indian songs and legends. A Plains Indian legend says that when humans first walked upon the prairie, Pasque flowers turned and said, "Good morning," but humans ignored them, so the flowers became shy. Today, they turn away and whisper silent greetings when people approach.

The Pasque flower is highly toxic, and while several Plains tribes used it for medicines, it had to be treated with respect, as too much could bring about vomiting, convulsions, and coma.

< 37 >

Wild turkey

Despite their weight, wild turkeys, unlike their domestic counterparts, are agile fliers. Their ideal habitat is an open woodland or savanna, where they may fly beneath the canopy top and find perches. An adult male turkey has 5,000 to 6,000 feathers, which protect, allow flight, and are used to display to potential mates. The more colorful feathers of the males are iridescent, with various shades of red, green, copper, bronze and gold. Turkey feathers were often a part of headdresses and clothing of some American Indian tribes, who sometimes burned portions of forests to create a habitat for the birds.

Movements of wild turkeys inspired the Caddo Indian tribe's Turkey Dance, *Nu ka oshun*, part of a yearly celebration with dances and songs about Caddo history. The most commonly told story about the origin of the Turkey Dance is that a hunter was in the woods when he heard beautiful songs. Following the sounds, he discovered a group of turkey hens dancing around a gobbler. He watched long enough to fix the dance in

< The Great Plains: Plum >

his memory and returned home to tell all about it. After that, the dance he described was used with songs composed to record the people's history. The dancing lasts a long time, but it must be finished before sundown, when turkeys go to roost for the night.

Cocklebur

The seeds of the Cocklebur are spread not by wind, but by hooked spines that allow it to attach itself to any animal that is passing.

The Swiss inventor of Velcro®, George de Mestral, while on a nature hike with his dog in 1948, became covered with burrs. It is unknown whether these burrs came from the cocklebur or one of several other possible plants, but we know that he looked at the specimens under a microscope, saw the tiny hooks that were so effective at clinging, and said, "I will design a unique, two-sided fastener, one side with stiff hooks like the burrs and the other side with soft loops like the fabric of my pants. I will call my invention 'velcro'—a combination of the word velour and crochet. It will rival the zipper in its ability to fasten." He did, and it did, and the rest, as we say, . . .

< 38 >

Walleye pike

Carnivorous throughout its life, the Walleye pike is a top predator where it occurs, and has been known to live as long as twenty-nine years. Its eyes, like those of lions, reflect white light, as the result of a layer of crystalline matter in the retina called the *tapetum lucidum*. This layer gives the fish the ability to see in low-light conditions. Preferring to feed at dawn or dusk, on cloudy days, or when the water is choppy from wind, Walleye pike take advantage of dark water to hunt for their prey.

Mexican hat

Mexican hat is a perennial member of the large Aster family, and is related to sunflowers, daisies, and the Purple coneflower, also known as *Echinacea*. It is a favorite in wildflower gardens, as it grows in any kind of soil, doesn't need special care, is brightly colored, and is very attractive to bees and butterflies.

The Cheyenne made a solution from its leaves and stems to treat poison ivy rashes and draw poison from rattlesnake bites, and it was also used to treat headaches, stomachaches, and fever.

< Secret Voices from the Forest - Volume II >

Grey myotis

The Grey myotis, a cave dwelling bat whose entire population exists in only eight or nine caves, occasionally needs to use other places for roost and maternity sites. Storm sewer systems in both Arkansas and Kansas have now been designated "critical habitat," and are protected by law.

Coneflower

The Coneflower, or *Echinacea augustifolia* is a common wildflower of the Daisy family found in eastern and central North America. It has a long history among American Indian tribes, who used it to treat a variety of ills, most often snake and insect bite and wounds.

Studies done by German physicians in the early 20th century showed that it works by increasing the number of white blood cells. Today it is a favorite remedy in the treatment of colds, flu and infections, and is used to reduce inflammation, boost the immune system and expedite the healing of wounds.

< 39 >

Squashvine Borer Moth

This rather pretty moth is the object of fear and loathing by growers of squash and pumpkins, as its larvae can cause total devastation to his crop before the gardener has an inkling anything is amiss.

In late spring, the female lays about two hundred tiny eggs—one at a time, rather than in a clump—at the base of each plant. A week or two later, the caterpillars emerge and bore into the stem, where they feed until the stem collapses and the plant dies.

Conscientious gardeners and organic growers employ many methods to combat these voracious eaters, including a product called BTK, short for *Bacillus thuringiensis kurstaki*, a soil-borne bacteria that targets moth larvae. Other methods include injecting with beneficial nematodes, covering the plants with floating row covers, or wrapping each stem with nylon stockings.

< The Great Plains: Plum >

THE IMPORTANCE OF GRASS

In 1887, the western portion of the Great Plains was described as "an arid and repulsive desert . . . a region of desolation and silence . . . [with] common characteristics of barrenness, inhospitality, and misery," in *A Study in Scarlet*, Arthur Conan Doyle's first Sherlock Holmes adventure. Peoples of the British Isles, and points east had been, for thousands of years, committed to removing as much of "wild" nature as they could. Great cities, housing millions of people, were already common throughout "the Old World," so to even contemplate migrating to an area where the only inhabitants were tribes of American Indians, never very great in number, and a few rough and hardy trappers, miners and pioneers, was nearly inconceivable.

Having lived in Utah for several years, I can see why the British, and other Europeans, would consider a place so different from their homelands as inhospitable. However, Doyle's description was not specifically about Utah, and included a large section of the Short-grass Prairie.

"Lush" is in the eye of the beholder. In the Chapter One introduction, it was mentioned that sub-surface life on the plains is more extensive than that above ground; indeed it has been referred to as "the poor person's tropical rainforest," because of the abundant and varied forms of life contained per cubic yard.

The majority of us may not be particularly into the world of creepy-crawlies, and probably figure, "Oh, what's the difference if I kill all these little things every time I take a step because there's so many of them, and I can't see them anyway." Nevertheless, it's worth remembering that in the greater scheme of things, humans are comparatively small, and can be wiped out just as easily.

How do we know there isn't a being so immense, compared to us, that we're unable to take in its entire form all at once, and who, should it take a "step," would wipe out millions of *us* at a crack? And while that idea takes us to a "what if?" place more appropriate to science fiction, it is already known that certain viruses have the capacity to do the job very well.

While we tend to loathe and fear these microscopic creatures, they, much more than we, hold the planet together—literally. They are what allow plants and animals to absorb nutrients. Without them, "higher" life forms, which have evolved to make use of their abilities, would not survive, and that includes us. Without all those microbes, bacteria, yeasts, and others, Earth would still be a big rock with a molten core, slowly cooling.

But the subject was grass. And the evolution of grasses, it appears to me, accounts for the great explosion of current life forms. Countless animals, of all sizes, eat them, and are eaten in turn, returning in death to the soil and, as a matter of fact, eventually *as* soil. So the little, humble things such as algae, bacteria, viruses, fungi, ants, bees, birds, and yes, grass, are important—actually, vital. Without any of them, life would all just fade away.

CHAPTER TWO

THE GREAT LAKES

ancient hills still guarding
lakes of living water
in this sacred bowl

⟩⟩⟩⟩⟩⟩⟩⟩⟩⟩⟨⟨⟨⟨⟨⟨⟨⟨⟨

THE GREAT LAKES

With a total surface area of over 94,000 square miles and a total volume of around 5,500 cubic miles, the Great Lakes form the largest group of freshwater lakes in the world. As a group, they contain over 20% of the world's surface fresh water, and 84% of North America's surface fresh water. The Lakes are connected to the Atlantic Ocean by the St. Lawrence Seaway, but they sit in a large depression called the Great Lakes Basin, a watershed area, into which runoff from rain and snow, as well as some rivers and streams, is channeled. The lakes have maintained a fairly constant water level since the final retreat of the glaciers. However, population of the area by humans has only been intensive over the last hundred years and, although only a small percentage is consumed as drinking water, some modern activities pose the potential of reducing water levels.

These five interconnected bodies of water were created by the repeated advancement and retreat of the Laurentian ice sheet. Its last episode, called the Wisconsin glaciation, occurred between 85,000 and 10,000 years ago. The glacier was up to two miles thick in some places, and so powerful that it scraped out the Basin, which filled with meltwater as the ice retreated. If seen in a cutaway, the basin has many craters, some larger and deeper than others. The largest of these became the Great Lakes.

But it's not as simple as that. Why didn't the glaciers scour out other areas equally as large? The answer lies in the process by which the continents are formed.

Four billion years ago, the Earth was much hotter, because it was still cooling from impacts by other astral bodies. Radioactivity levels were high, and the molten core of the planet had not cooled sufficiently to allow the Earth's crust to create any stable formations. This was the time on Earth prior to the appearance of life.

During this period, the cratons, or continental cores, were beginning to be formed (largely out of igneous, or once-molten rock, and metamorphic, which is rock that has been transformed by heat or pressure) repeatedly colliding and melding together. These great masses slowly moved as well, sometimes striking each other.

Around 1.2 million years ago, a 300 million-year-long continental collision began a series of mountain-building events affecting the entire eastern half of the North American continent. Ultimately, the Adirondack, Laurentian, and Appalachian mountain ranges were created, as well as the Llano Uplift, which is all the way south in what is now Texas. It is thought that one of the collateral effects of this was the Midcontinental Rift, a great tear which began to split the continent apart horizontally, where two tectonic plates had previously fused together; however, it failed, leaving behind a great valley. Most of the rift filled in with sediment, as much as six miles thick, and Lake Superior lies within its borders.

A large part of the Laurentian craton is a plateau called the Canadian Shield, after its basic shape—when the Greenland section is included, the formation looks like a warrior's shield. The Canadian Shield was the first part of North America to permanently sit above sea level, where it has remained, the greatest area of exposed rock in the world from such a long time ago, covering over three million square miles. It was originally an area of high mountains, up to 39,000 feet, with a great deal of volcanic activity. It has withstood many millions of years of erosion, so the volcanoes are all extinct, and the once lofty mountains are now rolling hills.

The glaciers had their greatest impact on the Shield area, crushing rock, scouring out most of the soil cover, and creating and filling the Great Lakes, as well as thousands of other impressions that are now smaller lakes.

Glaciers consist of snow, compressed over a long enough period of time to become ice. When the mass becomes large enough, and the slope of the land is steep enough, gravity and pressure allow the ice to move. Glaciers form only on land, as opposed to sea ice, and though there are several glaciers in mountains throughout the world, 99% of glacial ice is situated in ice sheets at the poles and Greenland. These are the largest reservoirs of fresh water on the planet.

The Great Lakes contain some 35,000 islands. Manitoulin Island and Isle Royale are the two largest islands in any inland body of water, and are big enough to have their own lakes. The area generally supports forests and wildlife, although many of the forests are second and third growth, because of extensive logging.

The Great Lakes region is now heavily populated, with great demands being put on this ecosystem's resources, and there are many political issues, as the borders of the lakes and their waters are shared, not only by millions of people and scores of cities, but by two adjacent countries. Over time, treaties and commissions have been established to regulate usage and disputes. Pollution and invasive species, primarily introduced through shipping, have caused many problems, but the national governments of both countries, as well as the governments of the respective provinces and states, are working together to remedy these difficulties.

⋞ BASSWOOD ⋟

REFLECTIONS on FORTITUDE

What Basswood Can Tell You About Itself

In a competitive world, you must have courage to survive, or even to be alive in the first place. *Fortitude* manifests by finding a niche that will give you a better chance. Existence should not simply be about struggle, after all. It is easy to see why it is called "the Web of Life," if you observe that everything intertwines. Indeed, most creatures evolved in relation to many factors, such as environmental conditions, weather, available resources, and a gap in the fabric of life-forms. Seen this way, the life-and-death struggle is about co-operation, and what would otherwise appear to be unfettered brutality acquires a sense of nobility.

Is it not more courageous to welcome Life, in all its beauty and pain, horror and magnificence, than it would be to simply surrender to superior forces, without even making the attempt to carry on? Weakness is easy, but it is also a spiritual dead end. It is quitting.

The way I have learned to survive is by making friends—in my particular case, the bees, and other small creatures. It is *their* planet, after all. If they agree to help you—and reciprocity is part of the agreement—then you can survive. My flowers are what I have to offer to these creatures, and my blossoms generate a bountiful quantity of sweet nectar that they find irresistible. Flowering involves a great surge of vital energy, emanating from my very heart.

Basswood's Place in the World

Being near the Great Lakes provides my species with increased humidity, of course, but there is also a difference in the air itself—a sense of great distances that the proximity to a substantial body of water can give. We find that lakes are kinder, as they do not carry the intense salts of the oceans.

My ancestors have taught me to let tempestuous forces pass by without taking notice of us or causing us harm. To be "just another tree" in a forest is not so hard, except in spring, when I can't help but show off. It is also harder to blend in when the space between me and other trees is too significant. This rather goes against the customary interpretation of fortitude, but whom would my extinction serve? I embrace the contradictory parts of myself. The options are far greater with multiple outlooks! I hope to pass on even more clever ways of doing this.

My species has noticed that changes come in waves. Groups of species come and go, as they are interdependent. Currently, the overall physical size of all species has diminished.

We talk to other trees in our neighborhood. Sometimes we engage in friendly banter about who looks the best, but we also pass along the happenings of the forest, be they auspicious or not. To you, it would seem as though the wind was passing through our leaves.

My family sees its place on Earth as supportive — *really*, we are not ambitious. We don't need to be tall, or heavy, or long-lived. Frankly, those things require making an effort we can't fathom. We are just happy to help create the fundamentals that allow others to achieve their ends, which allows for even greater diversity in the world.

There are trials and difficulties for all forms of life, but servitude is a state of mind — it is only denial and resistance that creates imprisonment.

Basswood's Message for Us

The human species is the "Opportunist Extraordinaire," always on the lookout for ways to make use of any circumstance, creature, or object. We trees admire this ability in you, although we think it should be tempered by caution, or your inner voice.

You have the dubious honor of contributing a focus of energy to the planet. Others have had this distinction in the past, and though their time here has been marked by great displays of power, their effects did not endure long after their passing. The wise among you understand compromise, seeing that it is possible to learn from one's opponents. We each only have a part of the whole picture. The more pieces we have, the more easily we obtain what we require.

You might find it helpful to understand that insects are the *true* Masters of Planet Earth. They don't appreciate the constant war being waged against them. They certainly understand that you, like other creatures, must consume life to avoid death, but there is a cruel streak in your destruction of great numbers of them at once.

What you do not comprehend is that the planet would not survive without them. It would serve you well to have a cooperative relationship with the other Kingdoms of the Earth, which you largely do not perceive as such, the Insects being only one example. The Plant Kingdom is another, which is something you are learning, though perhaps a bit late.

If you want to use your power of focusing to elevate your species further, spend more time examining dirt. Or clouds. These are mysteries worth exploring.

< 48 >

< Secret Voices from the Forest - Volume II >

CHRONICLES

< 49 >

American basswood, or *Tilia americana*, is a large, fast-growing, deciduous tree native to the eastern and middle parts of North America. It is also called the American linden, and is closely related to the European linden, which is commonly called the "Lime tree" in Great Britain. Although the European linden can live a thousand years, the North American species has only been known to reach the age of 200.

The linden's mythological symbolism reaches back beyond the modern era in Germanic and Slavic cultures. It was considered a "tree of justice," under which rural conflicts were

< The Great Lakes: Basswood >

resolved. German-American immigrants brought a linden tree from Germany in 1912, and in 1918 planted it to commemorate the end of World War I and symbolize their loyalty to America. The tree is still maintained by members of the family.

The American basswood has a pyramid shape, and large, heart-shaped leaves, making it a favorite ornamental or street tree. Because its wood is soft and easily worked, it has been a preferred choice for carving items as diverse as Viking shields, Medieval altarpieces, puppets and marionettes, wind instruments and electric guitar bodies. Its inner bark, or *bast*, was utilized by American Indians as fiber for weaving baskets and rope, made to bind up canoes and snowshoes.

Basswood flowers, fruits, and wood have been used in herbal remedies for thousands of years, for the treatment of a variety of ailments. At one time, flowers were even added to baths to aid in the treatment of hysteria (presumably manifesting in us frail women.)

Because of the large amount of nectar yielded by the flowers, the tree is a particular favorite of bees, who produce from it a high quality honey. *Tilia americana* is one of three flowering trees important as a nectar source for bees. The others are the Yellow poplar and the Black locust.

As a single source for nectar, basswood rivals clover, thistle and milkweed, providing the bees enough to produce 800-1,100 pounds of honey per acre. Since bees are hard to contain, beekeepers must know when nectar sources—trees, shrubs, flowering crops or herbs—are ready to bloom, and be ready to move hives into their vicinity.

If 80 percent of the content of a particular honey can be shown to be from one source, it can be considered a *monofloral* or *unifloral* honey. It is more highly valued than honey from mixed sources, and will be kept in separate, marked containers.

Some typical examples of North American monofloral honeys are clover, orange blossom, blueberry, sage, tupelo, buckwheat, fireweed, and sourwood, as well as the linden, or basswood. Each of these has different properties, and can be used either to fight or improve several medical conditions. Basswood, in particular, yields a strong-flavored, aromatic honey that aids against cold and flu, coughs, sinusitis, headache, sleeplessness and anxiety, relieves pain, and can help with the cleansing of the body by opening pores or aid with kidney problems by increasing the flow of urine.

The power of honey to heal was widely recognized in ancient times, and its use is well documented in Vedic, Greek, Roman, Christian, Islamic and other texts. The Egyptians used it both internally and externally to soothe burns and cuts, and to aid the healing of wounds and infections; by the Greeks and Romans, who made use of honey's antibacterial properties to dress battle wounds; and by practitioners of the traditional Hindu system of healing, Ayurveda. They believed that honey would create balance in all the bodily systems.

Raw, organic honey, that has not been pasteurized, has been proven to have antiseptic, anti-inflammatory and anti-fungal properties that do indeed help heal wounds. Some of the ailments that have been successfully treated include: burns and open wounds, diabetic ulcers (topically), migraines, insomnia, hyperactivity, anemia, osteoporosis, colds, fevers, sore throat, eczema, acne, inflammation of the gastrointestinal tract, indigestion, laryngitis, hay fever and asthma, to give a partial list. The only conditions in which honey is contraindicated are diabetes (if internally consumed), acute heart failure or pulmonary hemorrhage.

The results of modern clinical studies have been largely inconclusive, so honey is still considered part of "alternative" medicine. Despite this, because the quality of the honey used in the studies has not been regulated, research results could be considered invalid.

Many believe that the therapeutic possibilities of honey should be investigated further. However, as honey is a product of nature, it cannot be patented, and thorough studies are unlikely to be funded. It may remain for individuals to experiment with simple remedies, with the guidance of non-traditional healers, or by using common sense.

< 51 >

< The Great Lakes: Basswood >

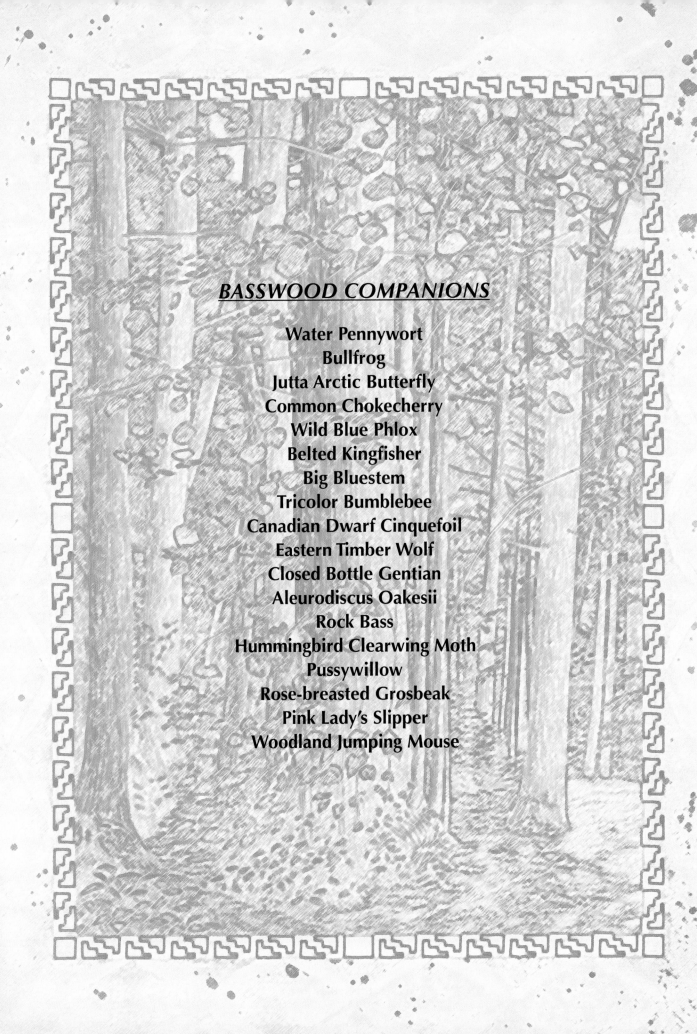

BASSWOOD COMPANIONS

Water Pennywort
Bullfrog
Jutta Arctic Butterfly
Common Chokecherry
Wild Blue Phlox
Belted Kingfisher
Big Bluestem
Tricolor Bumblebee
Canadian Dwarf Cinquefoil
Eastern Timber Wolf
Closed Bottle Gentian
Aleurodiscus Oakesii
Rock Bass
Hummingbird Clearwing Moth
Pussywillow
Rose-breasted Grosbeak
Pink Lady's Slipper
Woodland Jumping Mouse

Basswood has its bark torn off, its soft
inner tissue flayed with hooked blades,
tearing out fibers for ropes and baskets:
how useful!

       Linden remembers
       the first giving, the life-leap,
       and gives and gives again
       its own sweet nectar.

Basswood has its wood ripsawn
and quartered, machine-shaped for music's
sake, or carved by hand to a saint's
pious likeness:
how uplifting!

       Linden, large of heart, feels fellowship
       with all, eases where possible paths
       and the carried load.

Basswood remains are smashed and chipped,
force-fed to furnace, heat for the mighty:
how righteous!

       Linden lends shade for just
       reflection, comprehends both harm
       and heal, and holds the balance.

    (In the eon-vacant wind that blows
    we murmur render
    unto Caesar: render...)

Basswood: Tree of The World

       Linden: leaving for Light

FACTS ABOUT SOME BASSWOOD COMPANIONS

Belted Kingfisher

Belted Kingfishers dig burrows into earthen banks, usually near water, but they will make use of human-created areas, such as gravel pits, landfills or ditches. Both male and female of a mated pair will excavate a tunnel that is from one to eight feet long, sloping upwards from the entrance to keep water from collecting in the nearly spherical nest chamber.

Newly hatched Kingfishers' stomachs contain more acid than adults, which helps them digest all parts of the small animals brought to them to eat. By the time they leave the nest, this condition has changed and, like owls, they begin regurgitating pellets that contain bones, shells and other indigestible material.

American pussy willow

< 54 >

Many species of willow over the world are called "pussy willow," but in North America, the plant referred to by this name is *Salix discolor*. Most willows are dioecious, so catkins appear on both, but only the male catkins are covered in the familiar fine grey hairs.

Like other willows, the American pussy willow takes root easily from cuttings or broken branches, and is aggressively expansive, which is why willow trees of all species often line the banks of streams and rivers, where their roots hold the banks in place.

Willow bark is a source of *salicin*, which is metabolized into *salicylic acid*. Indian tribes all over the Americas used it for relief from pain, as its descendant, in the form of aspirin, is used today.

Because it is supple and less likely to split, willow wood has long been used in the making of baskets, brooms, tools, rope, paper and furniture. Today, because it has the capacity to filter out chemical toxins in the ground and water, it is being used in biofiltration systems and land reclamation.

Bullfrog

Its body, growing up to eight inches in length, makes the Bullfrog the largest frog in North America, and extended legs add another seven to ten inches. It can leap as far as six feet,

< Secret Voices from the Forest - Volume II >

so instead of catching prey with a long sticky tongue, the Bullfrog makes a powerful leap to ambush its prey. It feeds at night, and will eat anything it can fit into its mouth, including insects, birds, mice, snakes and fish.

A female bullfrog may lay as many as 25,000 tiny eggs that are held together in a sheet at the surface of the water. After hatching, the larvae can remain in tadpole stage for as long as two years. This makes for a larger adult frog, which increases its chance of survival.

Pink Lady's slipper

This perennial wildflower can live up to fifty years and grow four feet high, but unless the blossom completes its entire life cycle, the plant will not regenerate. The Pink lady's slipper takes many years to go from seed to maturity. Its seed does not contain any nutrients, requiring the threads of a soil fungus to break into it and pass on nutrients until it is more mature.

Pink lady's slippers also require bumblebees, or other strong insects, for pollination. Bumblebees are able to push themselves inside the flower, rub past the stamen to get out, and then spread pollen to other flowers. The fungus has a symbiotic relationship with the Pink lady's slipper, receiving nutrients from the roots of the orchid, but the bees are merely fooled by scent, and receive nothing for their efforts.

< 55 >

Eastern timber wolf

Wolves are social animals, living in a pack consisting of six to ten immediate family members. The pack needs a great deal of space, from 20 to 120 square miles. Neighboring packs may share a common border, but members of one pack, unless deliberately challenging the authority of another, will not venture more than a mile across the border. Specialized scent glands add a distinctive smell to border markings, as each wolf's scent is like none others—the same as our fingerprints.

Though the wolf is the dog's predecessor, the dog has lost some of its ancestor's "equipment," such as a jaw that opens more widely and has twice the crushing pressure, better night vision, sharper hearing, and a first digit that rotates, and can be used to clutch large prey.

< The Great Lakes: Basswood >

Big bluestem

Big bluestem grass is also called Turkey foot, because of the three branches at the end of each stalk. This most prevalent native grass of the Tallgrass Prairie can grow up to ten feet high. It has very deep roots and grows in dense bunches that prevent other grasses from taking hold in the soil. In the face of nearly constant wind, the soil of the prairie is held in place by plants like Big bluestem, which provide protection against erosion.

Because of this capacity, Big bluestem is currently planted to restore areas damaged by mining, road construction, and areas that have been over-farmed or over-grazed.

Hummingbird clearwing moth

If you have phlox, bee balm, honeysuckle, or dogbane in your garden, you may have seen *Hemaris thysbe*, but thought it was a small hummingbird. The Hummingbird clearwing moth can be understandably mistaken for its namesake, as it is of similar size and hovers over long-necked flowers, while emitting an audible hum.

< 56 >

Common chokecherry

Although their fruits are extremely tart, this widely distributed species of native cherry was the most important fruit in the diets of Northern Indian tribes. One particular way the chokecherry was used was in making pemmican, a dried mix of meat, fat and other ingredients. Other parts of the plant are quite toxic, because they trigger a release of prussic acid when in the stomach.

Chokecherries are of even greater importance to wildlife, providing food and cover to grouse, turkey and many songbirds, as well as fox, rabbits, raccoons, bears, deer and many small mammals.

Tricolor bumblebee

Before the introduction of European honeybees, bumblebees were the only honey-producing bees in North America, albeit they produced honey only in very small quantities.

< Secret Voices from the Forest - Volume II >

They are also important pollinators of flowering plants. Up to forty percent of the world's food production is due to pollination by wild bees. It has been found that bumblebees are particularly helpful in hothouse production of tomatoes, as the vibration of their flight muscles dislodges flower pollen, which results in more tomatoes.

The bumblebee queen builds the nest herself, usually underground. The colony never gets very large, often consisting of less than fifty bees.

Home gardeners who provide flowers and nesting sites for bumblebees also help adjacent agricultural land, as it has been found that bumble bees prefer not to nest in open fields.

Unlike a honeybee, the bumblebee does not lose its stinger after one use, but it won't usually sting people. Rather, it depends on its very loud buzz to intimidate.

Aleurodiscus oakesii

This small "crusty" fungus lives on the dead, outer bark of hardwood trees. Since the outer bark is not part of the nutritional transport system of the tree, no harm is done, although homeowners may find the resulting smooth patches unsightly.

The fruiting body of *Aleurodiscus oakesii* is more or less saucer-shaped, stemless, pale brown with white edges, and only about a half-inch across. As such, it is not often recognized by the amateur as a fungus.

"Aleuro" means flour, in reference to the white powdery appearance of the surface of the fungus, and "discus" to its shape. While it is understandably thought that "oakesii" refers to its preferred host, the oak tree, the name is, in fact, a deliberate pun made up by the mycologists who first described the fungus in 1873. They named it in honor of William Oakes (1799-1848), a famous lawyer-turned-Botanist from New England who collected the original specimen during a geological survey of the White Mountains of New Hampshire.

⪦ WHITE/BLACK SPRUCE ⪧

REFLECTIONS ON GENETIC MEMORY

What Spruce Can Tell You About Itself

All of those who preceded you are present within your own form; your body and its content are what they are today because of the interaction your ancestors had with changing environmental factors. This somatic code is not simply physical; it is composed of physical, mental, and emotional recollections. This is a method of survival known as *Genetic Memory*.

I am aware of a gathering of forebears within me. They see through my eyes, and yet, I am the New One that comes about through living in the present moment. This is the state of all things, really. There is a constant presence behind every living thing that appears as a "ghost of the past."

I dream of expansion and contraction—becoming corporeal, then insubstantial again, over and over. Sometimes when I expand, I find that I have taken a completely different form, such as when I was ice, and learned about being solid and unmoving, as part of an enormous glacier, or when I was a polar bear (hard to remember which came first), and got tired of killing to survive.

As part of these lifetimes, I chose to dwell near the Great Lakes. It was easier, in the quiet emptiness of the northern forests, to experience the greatness of the universe, and to shed self-concern and the notion of individuality. The lakes have a grounding presence, as they are located in an area where energy focuses, draining the distress and concerns of the moment away, running out into the oceans, where negative forces lose their sting. I feel it is important to become free of agitation.

Spruce's Place in the World

Members of my family, *Pinus*, are harbingers of the future. If you watch how it goes with us, you will see what lies ahead for you. We are also guides. We did not break the first ground; our job was to prepare the earth for those who followed us. Black and White spruces, so close as to be difficult to tell apart, favor simplicity and constancy. We are dependable. The two of us have also learned that comfort is unimportant, in the larger scheme of things, and that worms are under-appreciated!

Our ancestors taught us that Life is a great ocean, its waves moving slowly across the planet, in accord with its larger changes. When conditions favor, forms issue forth in a copious stream, filling every space, like a brimming cornucopia. As circumstances become less benign, Life may recede, reincorporating some forms, waiting for the next unfolding.

Of course, knowing that your time is coming to an end can be stressful but, since trees such as we often grow in a great, unbroken expanse, messages travel speedily from tree to tree through the branches. We are preparing ourselves for a resting time.

The spruces of the tree world know that pain is a test. Though particular incidents can be difficult, the ability to find a peaceful center within teaches us endurance, and freedom from fear. At the moment, changes are coming more quickly, so, it is a challenge to respond quickly enough — trees do not move at the same speed as you.

Spruce's Message for Us

You act like a great river that is flooding its banks, not really aware of those you pass or the banks you erode, so intent on the act of moving, that you sweep away anything and anyone in your path.

Your own Genetic Memory is unconscious, but *fully* in control. However, because of your potential for intelligence and self-awareness, you do have the capacity to bring forth other parts of your own code.

For instance, practicing altruism towards other species, by preserving and protecting the land as safe habitat for all, will benefit you, as you will then be able to see the effects of your present actions more clearly.

It is also important to build community that is based in close contact and resolution of difficulties through peaceful compromise. Put yourself in another's place to gain wisdom.

< 60 >

< Secret Voices from the Forest - Volume II >

CHRONICLES

Picea glauca and *Picea mariana*, members of the Pine family, both occur naturally in a wide band of continuous forests, stretching across all of North America. As long as these forests lie undisturbed, they will be the predominant species. However, as these trees easily burn, and destructive fires take place every 50 to 150 years, great age is rarely attained.

After a fire, an area is quickly populated with pioneering species such as aspen, birch and poplar. Stands of these are scattered throughout all but the oldest spruce forests, visible

< The Great Lakes: Spruce >

particularly in fall, when they turn bright shades of yellow, gold, orange and red. Both spruce species will grow beneath the shade of these deciduous trees, and eventually replace them.

As the last glacial period came to an end, great forests of cold-tolerant White spruce followed the withdrawal of the ice sheets, opening up the de-glaciated lands. At the same time, they began to disappear from the Great Plains, as the temperatures rose.

White and Black spruces are closely related, and it is often difficult to distinguish young trees of one species from the other, but there are several differences: White spruce grows taller, with a wider trunk, its shape is like that of a Christmas tree; Black spruce is short, with a bottle-brush shape that can appear stunted, due to the conditions of its common growing sites—wet, windy bogs. The white prefers to populate areas with somewhat drier, better-drained soils.

White spruce seeds are the food of choice of many small forest animals, particularly red squirrels. An individual squirrel may consume as many as two thousand seeds per day, some areas losing 90% of its seed crop to them.

Black spruce is a source of an essential oil that is considered beneficial in the restoration of depleted adrenal glands, as well as in the relief of poor circulation, rheumatism, and lung ailments, such as asthma, bronchitis and coughs. An ingredient in massage oil, it stimulates circulation and relieves muscular pain. Spruce essential oil is an antiseptic and cleansing agent or, simply used in a diffuser, will add a fresh scent to a room.

Early chewing gum was made from spruce resin, as well as medicines and a non-alcoholic beer. In more recent times, spruce has been used in the construction of pianos and violins.

Because of government restrictions on the use of wood during World War II, spruce was sometimes used in the construction of planes. Howard Hughes was asked by the government to design a massive plane, made entirely of wood, meant to carry troops and supplies during World War II. Though it was dubbed the "Spruce Goose" by the press, it was made almost entirely from birch.

< 62 >

< Secret Voices from the Forest - Volume II >

There are a lot of new words and phrases being used to describe planet Earth, some of them confusing or interchangeable. One of these words is *biome*, defined as "one of the world's major communities, classified according to the predominant vegetation and characterized by adaptations of organisms to that particular environment." There are six primary types of biomes: freshwater, marine water, desert, forest, grassland, and tundra, and each biome's dominant plants are determined by rainfall and climate.

The largest terrestrial biome is called the *taiga*, or *boreal forest*, containing some 30% of the world's forests, primarily located in Canada, northern Europe and Russia. The taiga has a long, cold winter and a short growing season of only one to four months. However, because this area is further north, the number of summer daylight hours increases as well, and many plants will begin growing at a lower temperature to take advantage of this.

The last glacial period lasted from 85,000, up to 10,000 years ago, covering most of the taiga with a thick ice sheet. When this period ended, the retreating ice radically altered the land, leaving behind deep holes and grooves. These filled with rain and melt water, creating lakes, rivers and low-lying areas that have become permanent bogs.

< 63 >

Forest makeup differs somewhat in each region. In North America, it consists mostly of coniferous trees, pine, fir, spruce and larch, with a few small-leaved deciduous trees such as birch, willow and aspen. A closed canopy forest is formed, with an understory of acid-loving shrubs, mosses and lichens. The northernmost regions of the taiga have fewer trees and more lichen ground cover; in the south, there is a gradual transition from taiga to temperate forests and grasslands.

Canada's boreal forest sustains many species of animals, including the Wood bison, moose and caribou, Canada lynx, Gray wolf, several species of bear, hundreds of species of birds and rodents, and many thousands of species of insects, crucial members of the system which act as pollinators and decomposers. Climate conditions make this a difficult biome for reptiles and amphibians, and only a few species are found.

The Canadian taiga, with its vast acreage of trees and, more importantly, large areas of peat, play an important role in the global carbon cycle: they contain 25–35% of the world's sequestered carbon. The release of this stored carbon to the atmosphere, due to either natural or human causes, would bring about profound alterations, not only to the boreal forest, but to the balance between the other planet biomes as well.

< The Great Lakes: Spruce >

WHITE/BLACK SPRUCE COMPANIONS

Muskellunge
Painted Trillium
Woodland Sedge
Star-nosed Mole
Yellow Warbler
Eastern Hophornbeam
Water Boatman
Blue Flag
Common Loon
Sneezeweed
Bronze Copper
Mudpuppy
Gomphus Clavatus
Shining Flat Sedge
Wood Turtle
Spotted Coralroot
Fisher
High Bush Blueberry

< 64 >

< Secret Voices from the Forest - Volume II >

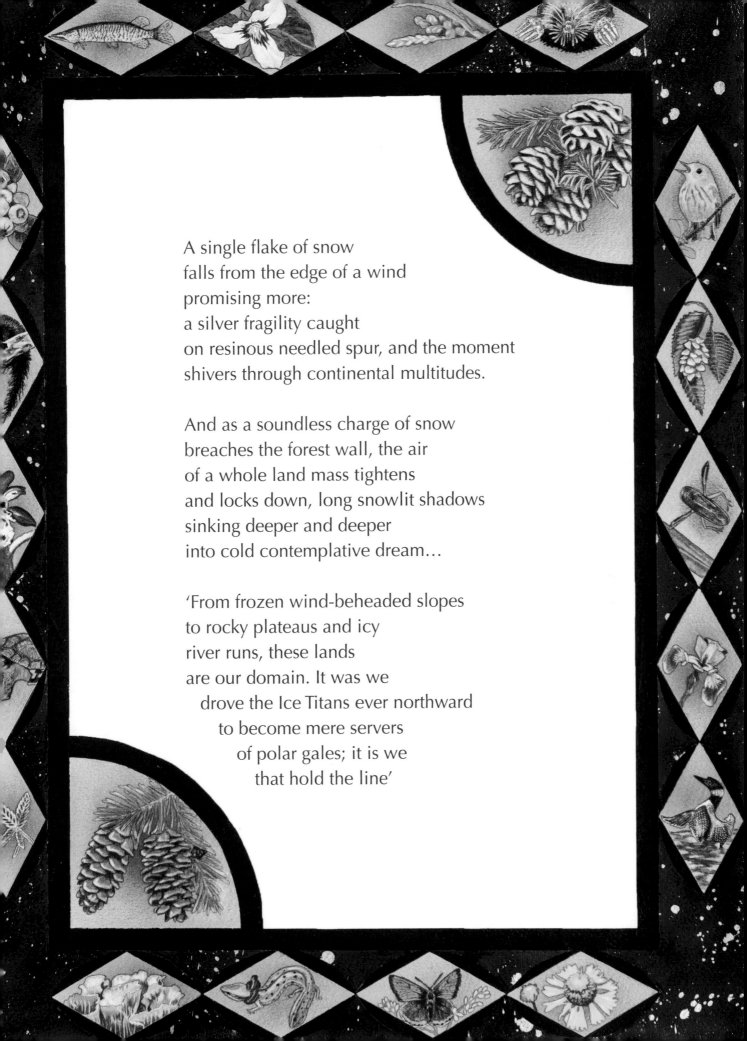

A single flake of snow
falls from the edge of a wind
promising more:
a silver fragility caught
on resinous needled spur, and the moment
shivers through continental multitudes.

And as a soundless charge of snow
breaches the forest wall, the air
of a whole land mass tightens
and locks down, long snowlit shadows
sinking deeper and deeper
into cold contemplative dream…

'From frozen wind-beheaded slopes
to rocky plateaus and icy
river runs, these lands
are our domain. It was we
   drove the Ice Titans ever northward
      to become mere servers
         of polar gales; it is we
            that hold the line'

FACTS ABOUT SOME SPRUCE COMPANIONS

Mudpuppy

One of the largest salamanders, at an average length of eleven inches, the Mud-puppy is so called because someone once thought it makes a dog-like barking sound, although this is apparently not the case. Its bright red external gills make it easy to recognize but, unlike many other salamanders, it never loses its gills, spending its entire life underwater, in shallow lakes and streams.

Sneezeweed

The common name for this pretty plant came from the Native Americans use of it to make snuff. Although native to North Amer-ica, it did not gain popularity in wildflower gardens until European plant breeders refined its qualities.

< 66 >

Common Loon

The Common Loon is anything but common. Loons are primarily water birds, agile underwater hunters who shoot through the water like torpedoes, making abrupt 180-degree turns with ease to follow the fish that are their prey. The red in their eyes helps them to see underwater.

Unlike most birds, whose bones are hollow, Loons have solid bones. This extra weight makes them less buoyant, helping them to dive as deep as 250 feet, and remain under-water to hunt. However, it also means that they need a long "runway" of 100 to 600 feet to become airborne, although once in the air, they can fly more than 75 mph.

Their legs are set far back on their bodies, which aids in swim-ming, but makes for awkward movement on land. This clumsy gait, along with the maniacal sound of their call, is why they were given their name.

< Secret Voices from the Forest - Volume II >

Highbush Blueberry

Everybody loves blueberries: birds, bees, bears, and of course, us. Before the Europeans arrived, sun-dried berries were used by American Indians in stews and soups, and in a simple baked pudding called Sautauthig. Historians believe this pudding was served at the first Thanksgiving feast.

The Highbush blueberry is the source of today's cultivated blueberries. Until the plant was introduced into Great Britain and other countries, bilberries, a close relative, were used for the same purposes.

Star-nosed mole

Being virtually blind, this unusual mole relies on its remarkable nose, a rose-colored ring of eleven pairs of fleshy, retractable tentacles, to find food. The star is less than a half-inch in diameter, but is much larger than the noses of other mole species, covering eight times the territory, with a higher density of sensory receptors. In fact, the nose of this mole is the most sensitive organ in the entire animal kingdom.

The Star-nosed mole's brain processes information at an exceptionally high rate, giving it the ability to decide if something is good to eat within 25 thousandths of a second. Approximately half the mole's brain is devoted to processing sensory information from its nose.

It also has the ability to smell underwater. The mole blows bubbles through its nostrils while underwater, at about the same speed other rodents sniff. When these bubbles come into contact with an object, molecules that impart smell mix with the air inside, so when the mole inhales, within the bubble, it "smells" what has been touched.

The tail of the Star-nosed mole is nearly as long as the combined length of its head and body. During winter, serving as a fat storage organ, it becomes swollen in size.

Spotted coralroot

Most coralroot orchids do not produce chlorophyll. To survive, they establish a parasitic relationship with fungi located within their roots, which break down and deliver nutrients.

< 67 >

< The Great Lakes: Spruce >

As a matter of fact, it is now theorized that *no* plant is capable of breaking down nutrients itself. Plants that are not capable of producing chlorophyll engage in complete parasitism; others may have a partial relationship with a fungus, such as that which exists between trees, which have a symbiotic relationship with fungus in the soil around their roots, called *mycorrhiza*. The exchange happens between the *mycelium*, the tiny fibers that are the growing element of the fungus, and the roots of the plant.

Water boatman

The tiny Water boatman is an air-breathing aquatic bug. It comes to the surface to take a breath; then when it submerges, it tucks an air bubble under a foreleg, to take along for a supply of oxygen.

Relative to its size, the Water boatman is the loudest animal on Earth. Its song is so loud that it is audible to a person walking near the water, even though 99% of the sound is lost in the transition from water to air. A team of French and Scottish scientists registered the Water boatman's song at up to 99.2 decibels, which is equivalent to the sound of a large orchestra heard from the front row. All that noise is made by the male, which rubs one part of its body across another to make its courtship song. The area involved is only about the width of a human hair.

< 68 >

Painted trillium

The Painted trillium takes 4 to 5 years to produce a single flower, but if the flower is removed, the whole plant could die. Its seeds contain a structure that attracts ants, which disperse the seeds throughout their tunnels, where they can take root.

Wood turtle

The Wood turtle did not get its name because it lives in the woods, but because its shell appears to have been sculpted *from* wood. A turtle's shell is made up of bone, covered in keratin—the same major component contained in human hair and nails. The top part of a turtle's shell is called a *carapace*. A turtle shell is an example of an *exoskeleton*, which means that the skel-

< Secret Voices from the Forest - Volume II >

eton is located outside of the body, rather than inside. The bones of the turtle's carapace are actually its vertebrae and ribs, which is why it can't crawl completely out of its shell.

Blue flag iris

Those who use flower essence therapy believe that because the curving petals of the Blue flag iris reminds us of the curves of a stringed instrument—and all that implies—taking Iris flower essence can put us in touch with the source of inspiration within ourselves, and foster creative expression.

Muskellunge

An adult Muskie will attack and consume almost any living animal—fish, ducks, mice, frogs, and even muskrats. They are the top predator in the food chain where they occur naturally. The source of their name is the Ojibwa word, *maashkinoozhe*, or "ugly pike."

< 69 >

Woodland Sedge

Sedges, a grouping of plants which superficially resemble grasses, belong to the genus Carex, whose species are all perennial, total in the thousands, and are distributed over most of the world. Their great number and variety are partially due to constant changes in chromosome evolution, considered the most dynamic of all flowering plants.

They typically grow in wet ground, and tolerate shade, and are often used in habitat restoration and sustainable landscaping. Stems with generally a triangular shape when cross-sectioned and leaves that are spirally arranged in sets of threes are features that distinguish sedges from grasses and rushes. Some well-known species of sedge include the water chestnut and the papyrus sedge, from which the Ancient Egyptian writing paper was made.

< The Great Lakes: Spruce >

⚞ STAGHORN SUMAC ⚟

REFLECTIONS ON AVANT-GARDE

What Sumac Can Tell You About Itself

You may think this term applies only to the arts, but from where, after all, does inspiration come? From the creative source of the Earth and stars, that which wills the inexorable advance of the seasons, and leaves them only partially predictable. This is the same force that causes the movement of ice, which presses forward, then retreats, altering the face of the earth as it passes. Is it not Nature that is personified by the Muses? Those who listen to this source find that they *must* take the lead, meeting the world head-on, in a spirit of inquisitiveness that follows the blossoming newness of time. They keep one step ahead, protecting those who require strength of numbers to be secure.

My species embodies the spirit of *Avant-garde*, forging out into the open fields, breaking ground, our bright displays of orange and red forming a phalanx that distracts and intimidates. We seem to be independent, but there are many creatures of the Earth and Air, not to mention those of the mind, such as fairies and elemental spirits, who support our efforts, and indeed, are in the forefront themselves, making ready a place for us, so that our undertakings will have a greater effect. Creating a link between beings, being strong and fruitful, this is the basis of transformation.

Sometimes there is an almost tropical atmosphere in the vicinity of the Great Lakes, or at least, it feels that way in summer. The ever-present humidity makes things so much more comfortable for me, as well as for other things, like mushrooms and other curious and beautiful fungi. They are always present, having an underground existence that is, for all intents and purposes, immortal, in spite of the brevity of their appearances above ground.

I sometimes dream I am part of a chorus of ladies reaching for the Moon, waving and dancing as it passes overhead. It was part of an ancient ritual, one that was performed in secret, to make connection. I can feel that we thought it was important, but were afraid of discovery by those who called us "pagans." Perhaps my red flower clusters are in memory of the cost of our actions, but, as it often is for plants, death only happens to individuals, not the fundamental essence.

Sumac's Place in the World

We have employed trial and error as a method of survival. You could refer to that as "butting your head against a wall till either the wall or your head breaks."

My family, the Cashew, has a bit of an unfriendly, untrusting attitude, and has many defenses, also my particular species is a little less aggressive, and has found that listening may be the strongest defense of them all.

Our job is to make the ground ready for the larger, longer-lived trees, to lay some cover so their seedlings can take root and become established. We get along well with other trees — *mostly* because we are listeners. They are older and have purposes we do not comprehend, but that doesn't matter very much to us. Besides, they like to talk, and to instruct.

Sumac's Message for Us

The Avant-garde manifests in your genius, whatever its field — in the arts and sciences, and in those minds that are plastic; in those who can see the potential of a thing, even though that thing does not exist in the present. Your role here is to reflect true spiritual progress because, although following inspiration is something that is natural to your species, the innovations and discoveries of your most inquisitive are sometimes exploited by less developed minds to promote the aims of fear.

It is important that you reach towards maturity as a group. It is no longer necessary to behave as tribal units. You may be individuals and altruistic at the same time. Your contribution, speed, has gone hand in hand with your evolution, for although your capacity to damage has increased, your ability to discover methods of curtailing and repairing damage has also advanced, and can be set in motion quickly.

You would do well to apply your caring, and these new methods to the land and the needs of all of its inhabitants, plant and animal alike. Although Nature seems to be engaged in constant warfare, in the end, all things work in accord.

CHRONICLES

Staghorn sumac is one of a number of related plants native to sub-tropical regions; it is one of the few occurring in the temperate zone. Some family members are poisonous, containing oils that cause many severe allergic reactions every year, such as Poison ivy, oak, and sumac. Poison sumac may be identified by its dense clusters of white berries called *drupes*, while the drupes of the Staghorn sumac are rich shades of red, orange, yellow, or even purple, sometimes all on the same plant. Some beekeepers still use dried sumac *bobs* — late Middle English meaning "bunch" or "cluster" — as smokers to pacify their bees.

The berries of several species of *Rhus* have long been used to make colorful dyes and medicines, for both internal and external complaints, in Middle-Eastern countries and Europe, as well as North America; the berries have been consumed as food and steeped in water and sweetened to make "lemonade" and wine.

The history of the word "sumac" can be traced back to the Arabic *summāq*, meaning "red." Forked branches and small hairs that densely cover the leafstalks and stems, giving them a velvety texture resembling antlers, gave rise to the common appellation "stag's horn."

This tree is relatively small, usually not more than twenty-five feet high. Sumacs can and do multiply by seed that is spread by animals. Once seeds have established, *cloning* can create large expanses on rocky hillsides, roadsides or unused fields. A large colony often originates with a single seed that was left behind in the droppings of a bird or mouse, but that plant may have died, leaving behind many suckers that grew and produced yet more cloned offspring.

The Xerxes Society named the Staghorn sumac to be of "special value to native and honey bees," as its flowers provide nectar and its dense thickets create secluded nest sites. The berries are eaten by more than thirty species of birds and, because they remain on the tree all year, are an important source of food to birds and mammals alike over the course of the winter.

As well as plantings to promote cover for wildlife, Staghorn sumac is often grown as an ornamental, as it grows quickly, suffers from relatively few diseases, is tolerant of drought and poor soils, and exhibits showy, bright orange foliage in the fall.

The many-seed fruits attract several species of butterfly, and are larval hosts for the graceful Luna moth, as well as bluebirds, robins, mockingbirds, thrush, ring-necked pheasants, mourning dove, ruffed grouse and bobwhite.

< 74 >

All parts of the plant have been used historically for making red, yellow and black dyes and inks, and as sumac is rich in tannin, extracts were used in fixing dyes and tanning hides.

Other members of the Sumac, or Cashew family, include cashew, pistachio and mango, although these tree species only occur naturally in subtropical areas — those regions bordering the tropics.

There have been many studies done on the health rewards of eating nuts such as pistachios and cashews, citing such benefits as protection from prostate and lung cancer, defense against heart disease, improvement in male reproductive health, prevention of cognitive decline and, because of high fiber and fat content, aid in weight loss.

< Secret Voices from the Forest - Volume II >

Cloning can be a hot topic, but plants have been doing it for . . . well, according to some, as long as there have *been* plants—all by themselves. The process, in the plant world, is called *vegetative propagation*. Nearly all roots are capable of this, and form underground extensions, such as suckers, tubers, rhizomes, corms or bulbs. Some stems can be formed above ground, such as runners on strawberry plants, or new growth on old stumps of trees. The Quaking aspen is well known for producing entire forests originating from a single plant, the individual stems emerging from one great mass of roots.

Another form of plant cloning is called *apomixis*, from the Greek *apo*, "away from," and *mixis*, "mingling." In this process, a plant produces a viable seed without fertilization.

Natural cloning in the animal kingdom, called *parthenogenesis*, is also common. It primarily occurs in the females of some species of insects, crustaceans, frogs, lizards and fish. This is an asexual form of reproduction, requiring no fertilization, which will always produce another female.

A number of familiar trees and fruits are artificially cloned regularly. Horticulturists often prefer vegetative propagation, as less time is needed to produce results, and the outcome is more predictable. The term "clone" is derived from the Ancient Greek word *klōn*, meaning "a slip or twig," referring to an agricultural process called *grafting*, the insertion of a single bud, called the *scion*, into a slit on a host, or *rootstock* plant, which can be of a different variety, or even species. Apple, peach, pear, avocado, walnut, pecan, and all kinds of citrus trees are reproduced by grafting, while grapes, blackberries, sugar cane, tea, vanilla, pineapple, plum, willow, maple and potato are propagated by simply planting a stem, or *cutting*, from the original plant.

< 75 >

< The Great Lakes: Sumac >

STAGHORN SUMAC COMPANIONS

Grass of Parnassus
Smooth Green Snake
Barn Swallow
Common Hoptree
Fire Pink
Snowshoe Hare
Nodding Bulrush
Northern Crescent
Eastern Forked Bluecurls
Diporeia Shrimp
Witch-hazel
Spotted Wintergreen
Northern Goshawk
Canada Lynx
Claveria Fumes
Walking Stick
Torrey's Rush
Spotted Salamander

The avant-garde?
They're kind of like scouts,
holy discontents; like early traders,
their vessels listing from the weight
of what was never seen before.

What do you think of the hats
we Sumac wear?
            (hats are important;
                they circle the crown chakra,
                gold for the kingly, ruby for love)
The fan of leaves like a Mexican brim,
the tall central flower spike, risen up
like an array of sensors,
a dish receiver,
testing the busy air.

Big colorful hats for the ceremony.

The bold perform their living dance
on the leading edge of life itself,
so we ask ourselves
what new steps can we try?
            beating them out
            on the drum
            of the earth

FACTS ABOUT SOME STAGHORN SUMAC COMPANIONS

Barn Swallow

What sets this species apart from all other North American swallows is its long, deeply forked tail. It effortlessly makes sharp turns at high speed, giving it the ability to catch flies and other insects in great numbers. While the Barn swallow usually hunts near the ground, it can be seen swooping and diving high in the air, following the paths of insects, late on a summer afternoon.

There is an Indian legend that explains how the swallow got his forked tail. The People wanted Fire, so Swallow stole it from the Sun, carrying the burning brand on his tail feathers.

Once nesting in caves, colonies of Barn swallows now use man-made structures almost exclusively for their mud nests.

Common hoptree

< 78 >

This northernmost representative of the Citrus family produces small flowers that smell like oranges. These are followed by flat, one-seeded fruit called *samara*, which were once used as a substitute for hops in brewing beer. This tree is a host for the larval stage of both the Tiger swallowtail butterfly and the rare Giant swallowtail, and is a favorite food of honeybees.

Spotted salamander

The Spotted Salamander is a burrowing animal, nocturnal, and is rarely seen except during breeding seasons. It requires pools of water present during winter rains, where the female lays large clumps of eggs, often in the proximity of algae. There is believed to be a symbiotic relationship between the algae and the salamander. The algae are provided with a safe place to live and grow, and in turn, they produce oxygen needed for embryonic development of the larvae.

< Secret Voices from the Forest - Volume II >

Grass of Parnassus

"Grass of Parnassus" is not a grass, but one species in a large family of flowering plants. It acquired the status of "honorary grass" because it was a favorite of the cattle that grazed on Mount Parnassus in ancient Greece. The Oracle of Delphi was at the foot of the mountain, and as the Oracle was sacred to Apollo, so Parnassus itself became associated with him, as well as the gods Dionysus and Pan, whose sacred place, the Corycian Cave, was located on its slopes.

The mountain was also said by some to be the home of the nine Muses, and was therefore associated with their gifts. The name "Parnassus" has been used as a metaphor for poetry, music, literature and learning.

Smooth green snake

The Smooth green snake is also called a grass snake. It relies on matching itself to its environment for protection from predators. Lacking venom, this snake is harmless to humans or larger animals in its environment.

Snakes are deaf to airborne sound waves, relying on vibrations, which reach their inner ears, to figure out their surroundings. When hunting, they turn their heads from side to side, finding prey with their tongues and an organ on the roof of the mouth that interprets chemical signals.

< 79 >

Nodding bulrush

Though called a rush, this plant is a soft-sided *sedge*, and the stems of all sedges are triangular in shape. If you haven't heard the rhyme to help you remember the difference between sedges and other plants, here it is: "Sedges have edges."

The Indians cut rushes for mats and thatching for their houses. The thatching is insulating and waterproof. Woven with grape vines, they form rafts a person can stand on and pole over water. Bulrush "shoes" helped hunters to walk over muddy flats without sinking in. Shredded rushes were used to make baskets, baby diapers, sleeping mats, skirts for the women and capes for the men.

< The Great Lakes: Sumac >

When mature, they are five to thirteen feet tall, and leaves are slender and grass-like. The plants are edible, and can be used as a vegetable or to make flour.

Canada lynx and Snowshoe hare

The Canada lynx is one half of a classic predator-prey relationship, the snowshoe hare being the other, as it comprises seventy-five percent of the lynx's diet. This means that their populations also move in tandem. Every ten years or so, the hare becomes scarce, most probably as a result of disease. A year or two later, the lynx's numbers also decrease dramatically, the numbers rising again when the hare population rebounds.

The lynx weighs twenty-five to thirty pounds, with long black ear tufts, a pronounced goatee, a four-inch stub tail, and very large feet that enable it to walk on top of deep, soft, snows.

Snowshoe hares make their home in dense coniferous forests of the mountains, avoiding open areas. Their fur is dark brown in summer, matching the deep shadows, but in winter they grow an entirely new coat of white hair, blending in with their surroundings.

There are several differences between hares and rabbits: hares are a bit larger, with typically longer ears and hind legs; rabbits burrow, hares live above ground; rabbits are born blind and furless, hares are born fully furred, eyes open, ready to run; when threatened, rabbits freeze, trying not to be seen, hares use their big feet to run away. Like the Lynx, Snowshoe hares have especially big, furry feet that help them move quickly over the top of snow.

Pipsissewa

The Creek Indians called the Spotted wintergreen "pipsisikweu," which means "breaks into small pieces," after the belief that it could break down gallstones and kidney stones. The plant has been employed for centuries to treat many ills, but as it is increasingly rare, it is best not to collect it from the wild.

Pipsissewa has been a traditional ingredient of root beer and is still included in several brands. The oil is a flavoring agent for dental preparations, especially if combined with menthol and eucalyptus. In the 19th century Alice Morse Earle wrote in *Old Time Gardens* that the word Pipsissewa is one of a few words from the Algonquin that is today used in the English language.

Walking stick

From the Ancient Greek *phasma*, meaning "a phantom," the Walking stick, or Stick insect, is a master at disappearing into its surroundings. This insect and its cousin, the Leaf insect, are normally green or brown. Also useful in self-protection is its ability to enter into a motionless state that can be maintained for a long period. The only predator from which the Walking stick has no defense is the bat, which hunts by echolocation.

Only certain species of animals can reproduce by parthenogenesis, most notably insects, but also reptiles, and it was recently discovered, sharks. This is the process by which an unfertilized egg produces an offspring.

Witch hazel

This native shrub contains large amounts of chemicals called tannins, astringents which have been used medicinally for centuries as treatment for pain, swelling and inflammation of the skin and eyes.

The name probably came from an Old English word, *wice*, meaning "bendable." When the folk tradition of using hazel twigs as divining rods followed English settlers to the New World, the new plant was called "Witch hazel," which also may have implied the plant was affiliated with witchcraft, much feared at the time.

< 81 >

< The Great Lakes: Sumac >

ON TALKING TO TREES

I'm from the Midwest, and I guess you never really lose your roots. After forty-five years, and two books about the inner "thoughts and dreams" of trees, when I hear anybody say—and I do more often than you'd think—"Oh, I've talked to trees for years," I roll my eyes, and think, "Uh-huh, right."

More than a little hypocritical, I know.

So perhaps you're thinking the same thing about *me*, or maybe you just wonder exactly what I mean when I say I "talk" to trees. In the introduction to *Secret Voices: The West*, I put forth the idea—not new—that animals other than man, *and plants*, communicate, and the only thing that separates us from this din of constant chatter is our minds; to be more precise, the human partiality for language.

If you consider what's behind language—emotions, desires, requirements, fears—you can see how it developed: say you're a primitive human, maybe a quarter or half million years ago, and you see something dangerous coming. It's still a ways off, so you make a loud vocalization as a warning. Fear in the voice has a recognizable quality, so any member of your tribe who doesn't have a death wish makes for the trees. But what if that danger is a Saber-toothed tiger, or something else that could climb? Wouldn't *that* have been nice to know!

So whoever is left after the attack thinks of a way to indicate *which* threat is coming, using distinctive vocalizations to differentiate between them. The varying sounds represent dissimilar things; in other words, they are *symbols*. And since survival often depended upon receiving a precise description of the nature of a threat, these symbols were agreed upon, remembered and passed on to future generations of the tribe. Voila! Language was born.

But these words, or symbols, don't always accomplish the desired intent. How many times have you had to "explain" what you meant? More words, more symbols. This is partly because unless you have a grasp of your language equivalent to Shakespeare's of English, you will often choose inadequate words; but more often than we'd like to admit, we say things we don't mean. In other words, we *choose* symbols that are at variance with our underlying emotions and motivations . . . and the one on the receiving end, somewhere inside, knows it—a child, or an animal, even more so.

The good news, for those of us who like to maintain our disguises, is that nowadays, we're all such devotees of the conscious mind that we can get away with denying any accusations of insincerity with a straight face. The bad news is that we end up expending a lot of mental energy "covering our tracks," and lose a lot of the joy of living in the present. "Be here now," as they say.

So what does all this have to do with talking to trees?

< 82 >

< Secret Voices from the Forest - Volume II >

The first thing you have to do is allow yourself to accept the concept that all living things—*all* living things, whether plants or animals, evolved in relation to everything else in their environment. Nothing is incongruous. Nothing just got dropped here, fully developed, because something out there thought it might be fun—no matter how weird it looks.

Once you've wrapped your head around that, it's a short step to realizing that each particular plant or animal must interact with the other plants and animals in its environment in order to acquire what it needs to survive. How does it do that?

Anyone who watched the PBS nature show, "What Plants Talk About," knows that although it's not the kind of communication human beings are used to, plants do indeed "talk" to other plants, *and* to insects, birds and microorganisms, sending out signals— that warn, that threaten, that invite—and the necessary responses transpire.

We've been hearing about dog whisperers and horse whisperers for years. These are people who communicate, on an emotional level, with animals. Usually called in to deal with troubled individuals, they speak in soothing, gentle voices, and yet give the animal a feeling of security that comes with being in the presence of authority. It seems like magic, but these practitioners are unlikely to label it as that. They are aware that it's not so much the words they use as the tone and emotion behind them. They *can't* lie, because the underlying emotions will communicate clearly—language does not matter.

< 83 >

When I first began to do "readings" on the trees, I wasn't sure how to go about it, so I just sat and waited for them to say something. Needless to say, *that* was a bust. After a while, I thought, "Hmm … trees don't speak English." Duh. So I looked for a go-between.

Pet owners will understand when I say that a dog who was once my companion, was more than a dog in many ways. He was, truly, my best friend, and the bond was extremely close, but I never thought to try to communicate with him in any other way than wordless emotions; so, at his passing, when he spoke to me (in my head, of course), just once, very clearly, it was a bit of a shock. The sound of it was so unlike my usual head noise that I have never doubted since that the occurrence was genuine.

Eventually, I thought to employ him as my go-between, which worked well. (I should mention here that the dog's name was TOL, which was an acronym for "Tree of Life," so he'd had experience with "tree-speak.") I guess the trees have gotten used to me, because I haven't needed him as an interpreter for some time.

The process is this: I ask a series of questions, the "answers" come as images, emotions, or concepts, often wordless, except for the particular tree's "subject," which is always a discernible word or phrase. Then I turn it all into prose that (hopefully) hangs together.

So roll your eyes—I would.

< The Great Lakes >

CHAPTER THREE

THE UPPER MIDWEST

*not only gametes
merge and mingle DNA,
so do continents*

≳≳≳≳≳≳≳≳≳≲≲≲≲≲≲≲≲

THE UPPER MIDWEST

The precise area of the Upper Midwest is not exact. As a matter of fact, there are some half-dozen more or less "official" definitions, but all of them include Minnesota, Wisconsin, and Michigan. A sub-title to this chapter could be "the Upper Mississippi River Basin," so I am *unofficially* including Iowa, Illinois, and the State of Missouri, north of the river of the same name. Much of this same area was, historically, part of the Tall-grass Prairie section of the Interior Plains, although that has largely vanished beneath concrete or the plow.

For simplicity's sake, since water flows downhill, we will say that most of the streams and rivers of the interior of the United States—that is to say, those east of the Rockies and west of the Appalachians—flow downwards into a central basin, or *watershed*, which eventually reaches the ocean. The central river of this watershed is the Mississippi.

< 86 >

Beginning in northern Minnesota, at Lake Itasca, it flows more than 2,300 miles, receiving water from tributaries in thirty-one states and two Canadian provinces, on its way to the Gulf of Mexico.

A large section of the Upper Mississippi Basin was not covered by the last glacier, and so escaped its scouring effects. Since what glaciers leave behind—silt, boulders, gravel, and sand—is called *drift*, this terrain is referred to as the *Driftless* area. Though the glacier didn't scrape the soil away and leave rubble in its wake, it did leave behind great quantities of water, in a body of water the size of the Great Salt Lake in Utah, all held in check only by an ice dam. When that melted, a flood of biblical proportions was released, cutting deep, narrow channels through the underlying rock.

This rock is of a sedimentary type—in this case, limestone and sandstone formed by sediment from mountain runoff and the remains of sea life from the vanished Interior Seaway of prehistoric times—so its stratified layers can be seen along a large section of the river, in canyons, steep *bluffs* reaching up six hundred feet high in places, and astonishingly beautiful, or precariously balanced formations, such as can be found in the *Dells of Wisconsin*. "Dells" is a distortion of dalles, from the French, for "narrows."

It almost goes without saying that humans have lived near, traveled on, and generally used the Mississippi River Basin system as an all-encompassing resource for thousands of years, but so have animals of all kinds. Three hundred and twenty-six species of North American birds follow these rivers on their migratory flights in spring and fall, as do migratory butterflies, such as the Monarch. More than 50 species of mammal, and 145 species of

< Secret Voices from the Forest - Volume II >

amphibians and reptiles, as well as many species of crustaceans, make the Mississippi their home, and 25% of North America's fish species live in its waters; of those 260-some species, at least 34 of them migrate as well.

About the only thing we can't control is the weather, and we certainly can't command the rain or snow to give us nice, gentle, and plentiful (but not *too* plentiful) precipitation. (We don't even seem to *predict* it very precisely, but that's a different subject!)

Part of the life of a river is flooding. When precipitation comes in greater quantity within a given period of time than the existing channel of a river can hold, the river flows over its banks onto adjacent ground. The more meandering the riverbed, and the higher the water in the river, the more land is flooded. The area that floods, but does not experience the river's current, is known as the *fringe* of a flood plain.

Because the floodplain contains large deposits of silt, over time it can become a very fertile area. These lands are a tempting place to farm, and large numbers of people often take up residence. But when the river floods, although the rewards are great, the cost in lives and property can be equally significant. In Ancient Egypt, the annual flooding of the Nile, which brought fertilizing sediment from the mountains down to the plains, was the main reason that civilization developed, as it allowed stable production of food crops. But the waters could only come into the fields; any further, and villages would be washed away. Not enough, and there would be famine. Since the building of the Aswan Dam in 1970, the Nile no longer floods, and farmers must use fertilizers on their crops.

Like the Nile, the Mississippi (and all its tributaries) has been dammed and diverted, deliberately straightened, or constricted by levees more and more over the last two centuries. Wetlands that may have held substantial quantities of water in the past have been drained and developed, resulting in more water going directly into the river, so that it flows more quickly. Rather than decreasing the incident of flooding, these practices actually make them more prevalent, as was warned by civil engineer Charles Ellet, as early as 1853. Communities in the Upper Mississippi region have experienced major flooding several times. The greatest volume of water came in 1844, but since there were few people in residence, there was little destruction; later, in 1965, floods killed 19, displaced 40,000, and caused $200 million in damages; further flood years have occurred in 1993, 2001, 2008, and again in 2011, each time with a bigger price tag, although downstream usually fares worse.

< 87 >

< The Upper Midwest >

⧼ WALNUT ⧽

REFLECTIONS on ATTENTION

What Walnut Can Tell You About Itself

I am particularly aware of my environment, and how I am situated within it, not so much as it relates to *me* at any given moment, but in a dimensional way. To have, or to be at *Attention* means to be present and alert, to be aware of spatial relationships, not simply physical ones, but those that are created by the *potential* of interaction and reaction between organisms.

There is a consciousness that this potential acquires. It makes decisions and communicates them to the unconscious of the two objects—whether organic or inorganic, it makes no difference. It is the personification of Space. If the relationship between the two things changes or ceases to exist, so does the consciousness.

In the same vein, it is here in the Upper Midwest that the continent begins to become aware of its own age. My species is not exclusive to this area, and in other parts, the Land seems to slumber; here, the Earth has just awakened to the presence of the Sky, and feels aroused.

I feel that it is important to leave your mark. We are tested every day by life, and I would wish that a record be made of significant changes or improvements. I feel the slow stretch of my bark growing, which gives me perspective on the passage of time that is more tangible than the movement of celestial bodies. Time only *seems* like it's divided into bits, just as we, as matter, have become discernible elements of the physical, self-image of the life force. In the mind of LIFE, all its elements are parts of a single entity.

I have learned, in past lives, that it is good to have friends, whether you are part of a flock of birds, or a drop of water or a snowflake. I'm not sure that I ever dream. After all, isn't dreaming simply encountering a dimension in which we experience an unfamiliar spatial relationship with familiar things?

Walnut's Place in the World

My family, Walnut, has learned that the Earth is beautiful, but not an easy place. Good chances to learn abound. Movement is like a treadmill—you always come back around to the place you started; the future is just something to worry about. Why do you care? Desire is a cranial activity, meaning it's all in the head; fate is another word for fatalistic!

The Walnut species is food, for everything and everyone. It's not something I resent, you understand, but it does put perspective on existence in general: you come, you go, and in the meantime, it's all about survival—somebody's, anyway. There is generally a physical hardness to those of my family, which is a result of being constantly called on to provide food. A certain defensive stance becomes necessary, to put the brakes on, so to speak. My particular species has perhaps become a bit more hardened than the others.

Trees all have their own brand of small talk, but my family prefers to speak of colors and how they change with the light and through their relation to their surrounding conditions. The only problem with being rooted to the ground is that one sometimes feels a bit static, and color changes prove that there is a connection to one's surroundings.

Over many centuries, we have watched flowers become very aggressive. It's almost as though they think they run the show by themselves! So, we like to keep them in their place by causing the grass to grow.

Walnut's Message for Us

In humans, Attention manifests in the wise, the totally free, and the very young. You are always moving, growing and changing. You could benefit from making more selective choices, but that would require knowledge of the outcome—which isn't possible. So do as you will, and indeed, who can say this is not the way it *should* be?

Your role here has been to counter or even redirect. There is nothing innately wrong with that, as everything needs an opposing force to be active and develop, or even evolve in the first place. In a sense, all things provide those opposing forces to *some*thing else. Generally, these changes take place over a long stretch of time—sometimes millions of years, and you push the limits. Again, this is not innately wrong, and has happened many times before. The Earth has many powerful forces, which have, in their turn, moved continents, raised mountains and flattened them again, extinguished life, and created the conditions by which it could begin again.

Although this is a planet where, literally, the strong survive, you have the capacity to make a place for the weaker of us. Prisons are not a deterrent to crime, and fear does not inspire love or respect. Form closer relationships with the rest of Earth's inhabitants; listen to their simple, but clear voices and then follow your hearts.

< 90 >

< Secret Voices from the Forest - Volume II >

CHRONICLES

< 91 >

Found in the Eastern half of North America, Black walnut is well known for strong, dark wood that is easy to shape. Because of the current value of lumber, trees are becoming scarcer, making wood even more prized. In the past, a piece of furniture would be made from solid walnut, but is now made from a less expensive kind of wood, then covered with a walnut veneer. A healthy 200-year-old tree with a straight trunk can be worth many thousands of dollars. As a result, incidences of tree "poaching" are becoming more common. In 2012, a man from Des Moines, Iowa was sentenced to fifteen months in jail, three years of supervised release, and restitution of $56,000 for the illegal removal of thirty-two Black walnut trees from public land.

< The Upper Midwest: Walnut >

Life forms evolve through their efforts to meet the challenges of their environment. Just as the walnut emits chemical toxins from its root system that inhibit the growth of competitors, all plants have developed defenses, not just to guard territory, but to keep from being devoured by bacteria, viruses, insects and grazing animals. The invaders come back with new weapons, and the plants respond with even more sophisticated deterrents. For instance, many viruses, while replicating, produce RNA or DNA strands that are alien to the targeted plant. The plant may respond in turn by digesting these foreign particles, turning them into useless fragments, thus halting the infection.

< 92 >

> Plants and animals evolved simultaneously from a common ancestor called *cyanobacteria*, also known as *blue-green algae*. Cyanobacteria are single-celled organisms, related to bacteria, but capable of photosynthesis. They are considered to represent the earliest form of life on earth.
>
> Hypotheses on how this original life began are varied, ranging from spontaneous emergence from a "primordial soup" to extraterrestrial seeding. As yet, there is no universally accepted theory on the beginning of life, but here is a *very* abbreviated scenario: primordial Planet Earth had almost no oxygen. There was a nice break of a billion years when there were no massive objects bombarding us, and the volcanoes had settled down a bit, allowing the Earth's surface to cool sufficiently for rudimentary forms of life to appear in the oceans. After another billion and a half years, single-cell photosynthesizing life forms appeared. The waste product of photosynthesis is oxygen, but it took another billion and a half or so years until the oxygen level in the oceans was sufficient for the emergence of life forms that were more than microscopic. Over the next 60 million years, in what is termed as "the Cambrian Explosion," multi-cellular oceanic life forms developed—although they are all now extinct—that were the evolutionary "stems" of some modern species, such as mollusks and arthropods. And that was before the *first* "extinction event."
>
> On Planet Earth, everything eventually dies, whether by disease, predation, or old age. If there were no death, the planet would have suffocated under the weight of living organisms eons ago. The only known organism to "defeat death" is the jellyfish *Turritopsis nutricula*, which is theoretically capable of indefinitely reverting to polyp stage after reaching sexual maturity, effectively achieving immortality.

The roots of Black walnut and other related species emit a substance known as *juglone*. It is toxic to many other plants, and kills or prohibits their growth. White birch, apple, red pine, and basswood trees, as well as many shrubs—blackberry, blueberry, azaleas and lilacs, for instance—and food crops, such as cabbage, peppers, tomatoes, potatoes

< Secret Voices from the Forest - Volume II >

and eggplant, will die if planted within fifty or sixty feet of a walnut tree. However, cherries, plums, squashes, melons, beans, carrots and corn are not harmed; they are perhaps even protected by their association with the walnut.

Like skin, which is *our* first line of defense against disease, plants have cell walls, waxy coatings, and bark. The development of these materials, because they give strength and rigidity, has not only given protection, but has also allowed some plants to achieve great size. In another defensive strategy, many plants emit organic compounds that either repel the assailant or attract something that will feed on *it*.

The nuts of the Black walnut are used in cooking and baking, and have been used in traditional medicines, often as a treatment for parasites; the shells are widely used in industry. Crushed to a powder, the resulting fine grit is used as a polishing medium for metals and plastics, cleaning jet engines, electronic circuit boards, ships and automobile gear, and making and maintaining seals in the drilling of oil wells. Walnut shells are mixed in with paints and varnishes for a textured effect like that achieved with a sand mix; they are used as a filler in dynamite, as well as an abrasive additive in soap, cosmetics and dental cleansers. A brownish-black indelible dye is produced from the shells, which is used in crafts or woodworking.

Most nuts are harvested by hand from wild trees. Trees begin bearing nuts at four to ten years, but reach maturity at twenty to thirty years, producing a large crop every other year. The State of Missouri's wild trees are the source of nearly seventy per cent of the twenty-five million pounds of walnuts consumed every year.

< 93 >

< The Upper Midwest: Walnut >

BLACK WALNUT COMPANIONS

Blue Jay
Switchgrass
Northern Pin Oak
Yellow Garden Spider
Yellow-bellied Sapsucker
Bunchberry Dogwood
Northern Prairie Skink
Cardinal Flower
Northern River Otter
Harebell
Great Horned Owl
Iowa Darter
Speckled Alder
Mycena Luteopallens
Harvester Butterfly
Eastern Wahoo
Ermine
Spring Larkspur

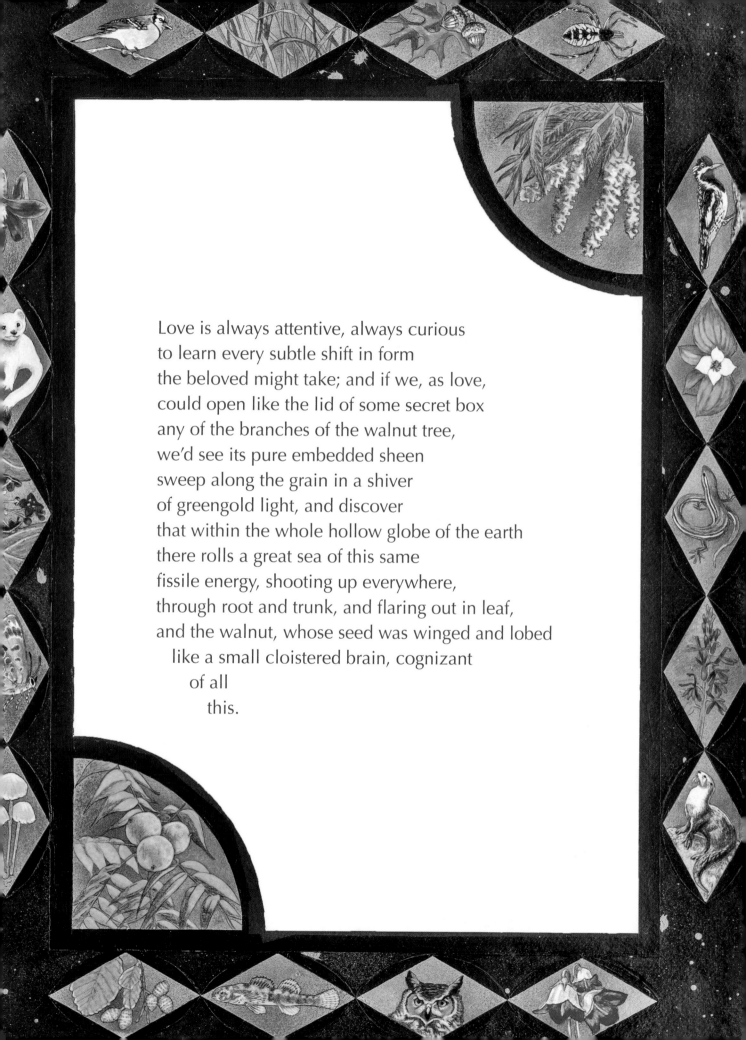

Love is always attentive, always curious
to learn every subtle shift in form
the beloved might take; and if we, as love,
could open like the lid of some secret box
any of the branches of the walnut tree,
we'd see its pure embedded sheen
sweep along the grain in a shiver
of greengold light, and discover
that within the whole hollow globe of the earth
there rolls a great sea of this same
fissile energy, shooting up everywhere,
through root and trunk, and flaring out in leaf,
and the walnut, whose seed was winged and lobed
   like a small cloistered brain, cognizant
      of all
         this.

FACTS ABOUT SOME BLACK WALNUT COMPANIONS

Great Horned Owl

The Great Horned Owl, the most common owl of the Americas, is found throughout North and Central America, and parts of South America. It is a *raptor*, or bird of prey, eating over 250 different kinds of animals, including other raptors, and it is the only animal that regularly eats skunks. Its strong legs and claws are powerful enough to carry animals two or three times heavier than itself.

To most American Indian tribes, owls symbolize death, and are said to carry messages or warnings from beyond the grave, but to the Hopi, the Great Horned Owl, *Mongwu*, is "a humorless lawman playing the role of 'straight man' to the Koshari clown," a prankster, and the father of the Kachina.

< 96 >

Spring Larkspur

The Spring larkspur is a *delphinium*, the name derived from the Latin for "dolphin", referring to the shape of its *nectary*. A nectary is a glandular structure that secretes sugar-rich liquid nectar from an atypical part of a plant. In some plants, these structures are more or less internal, so that bees or other insects must brush past the reproductive structures to access the nectar.

The Spring larkspur is a type of flower whose nectaries are located externally, and are not involved in pollination. These *extrafloral* nectaries attract predatory insects that will eat both the nectar and any plant-eating insects around, thus functioning as "bodyguards." These bodyguards are participating in a relationship with the plant that is called *mutualism*, in which two organisms of different species derive a benefit from the relationship.

Mutualism is important in ecosystem functioning, as more than 48% of land plants rely on relationships with fungi to provide them with necessary nutrients. It is believed by an increasing number of scientists that mutualism was the driving force behind much of the biological diversity we now see.

< Secret Voices from the Forest - Volume II >

Yellow garden spider

Yellow garden spiders are found throughout most of the United States. They are orb-weaving spiders, spinning their webs in circular, spiral patterns. Orb-weavers have an extra claw on each foot, to handle the threads while spinning. They prefer sunny places with as little wind as possible to build their webs. The web of this spider spirals out from the center and can be two feet across. The female builds the large web, and a male will build a smaller web on the outer part of her web. The male's web is a thick zigzag of white silk.

The spider had various meanings—it could be a trickster, a creator, or an intercessor between gods and man. Here is an Osage legend, which teaches that smaller doesn't mean less significant:

"The Spider and the People"

One day, the chief of the Isolated Earth people was hunting in the forest. He was also hunting for a symbol to give life to his people. He came upon the tracks of a huge stag. The chief became very excited.

"Grandfather Deer," he said, "surely you will show yourself. You are going to become the symbol of my people." He began to follow the tracks. His eyes were on nothing else as he followed those tracks, and he ran faster and faster through the forest. Suddenly, he ran right into a huge spider's web that had been strung between the trees, across the trail. When he got up off the ground, he was very angry. He struck at the spider sitting at the edge of the web. But the spider jumped out of reach. Then the spider spoke to the man. "Grandson," the spider said, "why do you run through the woods looking at nothing but the ground?"

The chief felt foolish, but he had to answer the spider. "I was following the tracks of a great deer," the chief said. "I am seeking a symbol of strength for my people."

"I can be such a symbol to you, "said the spider.

"How can you be a symbol of strength?" said the chief. "You are small and weak, and I didn't even see you as I followed the great Deer."

"Grandson," said the spider, "look upon me. I am patient. I watch and I wait. Then all things come to me. If your people learn this, they will be strong indeed."

The chief saw that this was so. Thus the Spider became one of the symbols of the people.

Canadian bunchberry

The Canadian bunchberry is also called the Bunchberry dogwood, and it has a similar appear-

< 97 >

< The Upper Midwest: Walnut >

ance, though it is a ground-hugging plant and the flowers are much smaller. The flower, which is actually a tiny cluster of yellow-green heads, is in the center of four white, petal-like *bracts*, or modified leaves. In late summer, bright red berries form where the tiny flowers once were.

The bunchberry has an impressive method of pollination: when an insect brushes against tiny antennae near the tip of the petals, an explosion of pollen is triggered. In less than half a millisecond, at two to three thousand times the force of gravity, pollen is flung out, where it either sticks to passing insects or gets carried away by the wind.

Switchgrass

Switchgrass is a native perennial that has been largely displaced by commercial crops, but studies are currently underway to discover if this, and other "biomass" fuels—defined by the American Heritage Society as "renewable organic materials, such as wood, agricultural crops or wastes, and municipal wastes, especially when used as a source of fuel or energy"—could take the place of corn and soybeans as a source for ethanol, since Switchgrass could be grown on soils too poor for food crop production.

< 98 >

Ermine

Ermine is the name given to the Stoat, or Short-tailed weasel in its white winter coat. During warm months it is a chocolate brown, with a white underbelly and a black tip on the tail.

It is an aggressive and adaptable hunter, in the wild eating insects, birds, rodents and other small mammals, some of them larger than itself. Five to seven million years ago, when northern forests were replaced by open grassland, there was a sudden evolution of small burrowing rodents. The stoat's ancestors went through a reduction in size at that time, which enabled them to take advantage of this new, abundant food source. Because it lived in burrows itself and could easily tunnel through snow, it was a successful species during the last glacial period.

Males and females live near each other, but not in the same dens. The female is the only active parent to the litter of kits, which are blind, deaf, toothless, nearly hairless and only a half an ounce at birth. After three weeks, teeth emerge; after four weeks, solid food is eaten; the eyes open after five or six weeks, and lactation ends after 12 weeks. Though male kits are sexually mature after ten or eleven months, the females are sexually mature at the age of two to three weeks, while they are still blind, deaf and hairless, and are usually mated before they have been weaned.

< Secret Voices from the Forest - Volume II >

The snowy white fur of the Ermine is a symbol of royalty and purity. There is an Indian legend that tells of an old man who had gotten himself into trouble with a powerful nature spirit after killing three little bears who were not old enough to care for themselves. He was given aid by the Old Woman of the Fairy Blue Mountain, who sent him the Ermine to kill the vengeful spirit. The Ermine's requested payment for his services was to have his brown coat turned snow white, so that he could be clean. The man used the wand the Old Woman had given him to grant the Ermine's wish, and he, in turn, dispatched the unforgiving enemy, after exacting a promise from the man that he would never again kill young bear cubs when they are still following their mother.

Blue Jay

The Blue Jay has a reputation for being a nest-robber, but close observation has revealed that other birds' nestlings and eggs are very rarely bothered. The usual diet consists of about twenty percent insects and small animals, and the rest seeds, fruit and nuts.

The Jay is particularly fond of acorns. It will often *cache*, or bury acorns for later, then never go back to get them. Because it carries food in its throat and upper esophagus, it can carry as many as five acorns at a time. Six monitored Blue Jays were seen to have each cached 3000 to 5000 acorns in a single fall season. The spread of oak trees after the retreat of glaciers, around 12,500 years ago, is partially attributed to the habit of caching by Blue Jays.

Harebell

While this plant is also called "Bluebell" in Scotland, where it was used to make blue dye for the tartans of the MacDonald clan, the Harebell does not carry that name in North America.

The Haida Indians of the Pacific Northwest called the Harebell the "blue rain flower." Children were warned not to pick it, or there would be rain. The Navajo rubbed it on their bodies for protection against witchcraft, and dried flowers were burned as part of a *smudge stick*, to cure the sick of ills that had a supernatural cause.

≼ RED MULBERRY ≽

REFLECTIONS ON CONTEMPLATION

What Mulberry Can Tell You About Itself

I get the greatest pleasure from traversing the vastness of the inner mind. There, time does not drag, and space does not limit. There, I am able to pause, to *Contemplate*, to look upon the wonder of life with admiration.

When I give shade and a place to rest, I am a facilitator to those who wish to join me in my meditations, whether the beauty they comprehend is in a well-contrived creation of man, or the guileless work of Nature. In this way, I hope to pass on an apprehension of the sublime.

There is an enthusiasm that is incorporated into the land of the Upper Midwest. It is the anticipation of transition — whether of seasonal changes, variations in the Earth itself, or the passing migrations of birds. I, myself, was once in the body of a migrating Canada Goose, and through that I learned that one must be obedient to the bidding of Nature.

It is important to consider all things as equally important in Life's design — otherwise, why does anything exist? To regard any of us as less significant is to imply dissatisfaction, which is not the case — for me, at least.

I don't think there is a difference between dreams and reality. I might like to experience flying again, as I once was able, but am more than content with my attachment to the Earth, where I can experience its wisdom firsthand. I can feel how the elements make themselves known — the air moves as wind, bringing the rain, which gives refreshment and life; fire clears a path for the new, and earth contains and creates a birthing chamber for all.

Mulberry's Place in the World

We were once all the same and together in one place, but as the land has moved and fragmented, we have become different from one another, as we have been unable to communicate by touch. Still, we can hear thoughts, and speak with each other about the sounds made by everything around us — from the wind, the birds and the insects, to the tiny organisms in the soil around our roots. They all have their own unique voices from which they can be easily recognized. We trees all agree that it is wiser to listen, and more prudent to refrain from speaking without consideration.

My family, the Mulberry, is one in the crowd, a humble inhabitant of the woods. We prefer not to stand alone, but in a neighborhood. Within those environs, we work with our allies to make a home for others, provide food, or simply make the earth stable. My species has learned that this planet has a soft and gentle side, which is experienced as a pause before storms, while the wind considers what direction to take next.

The Mulberries know and understand the essence of Truth. This is why so many want to consume us, though they may do it without knowing the reason. My particular species, the Red mulberry, radiates this knowledge in a pulsing wave that is like a heart beat. It makes us more adventurous, as with every pulse, our consciousness moves out further into the world.

Mulberry's Message to Us

You have set a goal for yourselves: to achieve elevation above conflict; to be at peace. What you are attempting to learn is that one can be at peace at any time, in any place, simply through acceptance of circumstances, and . . . this is important . . . by *blessing* them.

It is possible that you could achieve this goal more quickly by daydreaming, when inspiration comes to the surface. It is quite feasible to function and interact while in a contemplative state. This will allow new states of consciousness to be cemented into habit. It is not necessary to follow every thought, as most do not have conclusions. Calm your minds — this is the way in which humanity has its own direct contact with the Divine.

< 102 >

< Secret Voices from the Forest - Volume II >

CHRONICLES

There are a dozen or so species of mulberry, native to several continents. Red mulberry is found in the eastern half of North America, where its sweet fruits have been eaten by man, beast and bird for centuries. Taking the form of many small drupes, or fleshy, seeded fruits, each developing from individual tiny flowers, the berries, similar to blackberries, are red to dark purple. Many American Indian tribes used the fruits in food and drink, and the European settlers quickly followed suit, planting mulberry trees for use as food for both humans and livestock. Mulberries are still used extensively—eaten raw, used in baking and juicing, and made into wine.

Red mulberry has large, heart-shaped leaves, often with two or three lobes, a variability characteristic of new leaves. While mulberry generally has male and female parts on

< The Upper Midwest: Mulberry >

separate trees, flowers of both sexes can often be found on the same tree, but on separate branches.

The pollen from male trees can cause severe pulmonary issues, ranging from hay fever to asthma.

Leaves, twigs and berries have also been used to make dyes, and all parts of the mulberry tree have had a place in traditional pharmacopeia as a remedy for internal and external parasites, intestinal conditions and urinary tract disorders.

White mulberry trees were introduced from Asia in the 1600s in order to establish a North American silk industry, but in the 1800s, these plantations were killed by cold winters and disease. Later, seeds were imported again to promote a potential silk industry. While a North American silk trade never materialized, the White mulberry has since escaped cultivation and become naturalized in this continent. There is now some concern that the genetic content of the Red mulberry will be lost due to the ease with which it hybridizes with the Asian species. In Canada, the Red mulberry is listed as an endangered species.

Mulberries and other fruits and vegetables contain pigments called anthocyanins, which give them their red, blue, and purple colors. Plants rich in anthocyanins include blueberry, cranberry, bilberry, black and red raspberries, blackberries, blackcurrant, cherry, eggplant, black rice, certain grapes, red cabbage, black soybeans, and the Amazon palmberry, known as açaí.

Scientific investigation into the effects of these compounds on cell *pathology* (the behavior of disease) has led researchers to believe that anthocyanins can be useful in the prevention of heart disease and some cancers. However, until recently, promising results have only been obtained in laboratories. Human studies began in 2007, so it will be some years before research-based proof of the health benefits of these compounds is available, let alone drugs developed that

< 104 >

< Secret Voices from the Forest - Volume II >

mimic the effects of compounds that are produced naturally by plants. Until then, we could . . . well, just *eat* them.

So why do plants display all these bright, beautiful colors? Enticing as it is to believe they do it just for us, the function of color in plants is more straightforward, and yet much more complicated. The main reason plants have color is because of pigments within their cells. There are three primary pigments: chlorophyll (green), carotenoids (yellow, orange and brown), and anthocyanins (red, blue and purple). Each pigment absorbs wavelengths of light within a certain spectrum, while reflecting others. Light that has been absorbed will be used to power chemical reactions; the reflected light dictates the visible color.

It has been observed that plants requiring pollination often have brightly colored flowers and fruits. Sometimes the color is geared to the favored pollinator—hummingbirds are attracted to red, pink and fuchsia, butterflies like all warm, bright colors, and some bats and moths visit white flowers at night. Bees, attracted to smells and shapes, as well as colors, tend to prefer bright blues and violets, and carry out a large percentage of all crop pollination. Plants that pollinate by wind and air are often colored darker, as they do not need to attract insects and birds.

The same holds true for brightly colored fruits, which are more attractive to birds and animals that eat them, then spread the plants' seeds over great distances.

< 105 >

Because of their ability to convert light energy into electrical energy, anthocyanins have been used in organic solar cells. Solar electricity is one of the hoped-for solutions to the world's energy problems, but until recently, the expense of the technology has made common use prohibitive. Using the photosynthesizing abilities of plant pigments as their model, researchers have been developing *Dye-sensitized solar cells*, which use, as their basis, a non-corrosive, transparent gel that absorbs sunlight. The resulting product is a flexible film that is easier and much less expensive to produce and has a wider potential of applications than the stiff, heavy solar panels commonly used.

< The Upper Midwest: Mulberry >

RED MULBERRY COMPANIONS

Buttonbush
Great Spangled Fritillary
Mallard Duck
Common Prickly Ash
Wild Hyacinth
American Goldfinch
Trout Lily
White-tailed Deer
Garden Coreopsis
Red-sided Garter Snake
Ohio Spiderwort
Clitocybe Nude
Canada Goose
Blanding's Turtle
Eastern White Pine
Arctic Shrew
Northern Pitcher Plant
Giant Stag Beetle

With some difficulty we made our way through the outer fortifications, craggy and creviced as they are, populous and dangerous, until finding a natural breach through which we could pass.

We were then in a place of ceaseless industry, where everything needful to the maintenance and repair of the outer structure went on by day and night. We were not noticed and continued unhindered toward a further barrier, but this of a marvellous kind: it was an ever-descending gate, horizon-wide which, upon nearing it, we saw to be a latticework of crystals, intricate as a maze, each glowing a dark, nutrient green at its core.

We were able to step singly through the gate's slowly changing pattern and were at once enfolded in a region of softly tangled vines which swelled and burst in gentle peristaltic waves, the purpose of which we could not fathom. Pressing on, we were afforded a sight that mesmerised us utterly: it was a vertical river, blind, towering, siphoning slowly upwards from unknowable depth to unreachable height.

We might have tarried there in quiet bliss for ever, so it was with some effort we freed our gaze in order to penetrate through the viscous stream. We found ourselves then looking out over a vast banded plain, stretching beyond sight, alternating light and dark, dormancy and growth; each pair a life; a coming, a going, a re-birth.

Then it came to us that these were not rings within a plain but the unending orbits of planetary bodies, sweeping with wild energy through star-strung space, sung to their great arcs by a silent, magnetic core:

The invisible radiance of being

Creation's after-flash

FACTS ABOUT SOME RED MULBERRY COMPANIONS

Northern pitcher plant

Pitcher plants prefer the acidic environment of a peat bog, which is generally considered infertile. A large part of the reason for this is that peat, often referred to as *sphagnum* moss, puts out hydrogen in exchange for other nutrients. Increased hydrogen acidifies the pH of the body of water, making it inhospitable for most other plants, which need nutrients that are no longer available in a bog condition.

Unique species have evolved to become part of these surroundings, such as cranberries, blueberries, bayberry, heath, azaleas, wintergreen, and pitcher plants, which have developed a remarkable method of survival: all pitcher plants are carnivorous.

Insects such as ants, flies, spiders and moths enter a liquid-containing cavity, and are unable to escape. There they drown, and are digested, providing nitrogen and phosphorus to the Pitcher plant that its environment does not supply. The plant secretes enzymes that digest some of the insects that are caught. What remains are consumed by the plant's internal bacterial community. Larvae of a certain mosquito and midge, who develop within the plant, also eat some of the insects, and their waste supplies the plant with the rest of the nutrients it needs.

< 108 >

White-tailed deer

Although most of their natural predators have been eliminated, White-tailed deer can sprint up to thirty miles per hour, leap as high as ten feet and as far as thirty feet in a single bound—defensive capabilities that have allowed them to populate southern Canada, most of the United States and Central America, and South America, all the way to Bolivia. However, an individual deer's home range is less than a square mile.

Because of their abundance, White-tailed deer make an impact on the composition of plant communities. Seedlings can be eaten to the ground, eliminating new growth of forest trees, and in winter, they can kill large trees by eating the bark all the way around.

Like sheep, cattle, goats, llamas, camels, and giraffes, deer are ruminants, with four-chambered stomachs, each chamber having a different and specific function that allows deer to quickly eat a variety of different food, and digest it at a later time when it feels safe. Their stomachs are host to a complex set of bacteria that change as theirs diet changes through the seasons. If the bacteria necessary for digestion of a particular food are absent, it will not be digested.

When their fawns are first born, does are extremely careful to keep them well

< Secret Voices from the Forest - Volume II >

hidden. Fawns will lie for hours without moving, waiting for their mothers to return from foraging, withholding their urine and feces. When the doe arrives, she will ingest whatever her fawn needs to eliminate, so that no evidence is left for predators. The fawn of the White-tailed deer can walk at birth. It will begin to forage for food within two or three days, and is fully ruminant at two months old.

Eastern white pine

Pine tar, produced by slowly burning roots, branches, or small trunks of the Eastern white pine, has had many uses. Apparently, Pine tar mixed with beer can be used to remove tapeworms and round worms. Mixed with sulfur in a shampoo, it is used to treat dandruff, or processed to make turpentine..

Mallard Duck

The Mallard duck is believed to be the most abundant duck on earth. It is wide-ranging, attracted to bodies of water that contain aquatic vegetation, including city parks.

Since 1933, The Peabody Hotel in Downtown Memphis, Tennessee has kept one Mallard drake and four hens as an attraction for their guests. A trainer leads them in a march around the lobby and its travertine marble fountain twice a day, at 11 a.m. and 5 p.m. When the ducks are not on duty, they live in their "Royal Duck Palace" on the hotel's rooftop. A local farmer provides the ducks to the Hotel, replacing them with a new team every three months.

< 109 >

"Duck is not served anywhere at The Peabody, and has not been seen on the hotel's menus since its 1981 reopening, quite possibly making Chez Philippe the only French restaurant in the world that does not serve duck."

Garden coreopsis

Garden coreopsis is also called Calliopsis, which is Latin for "having beautiful eyes." It is a flower of the Composite family, whose members are found nearly everywhere except Antarctica. Nearly ten per cent of all flowering plants have composite flowers, including sunflowers, asters, daisies, dandelions, dahlias, and lettuce. A composite flower looks like a single flower, but is actually composed of many small flowers clustered together. Over 21,000 species of herbs, wildflowers, and shrubs represent the Composite family worldwide.

< The Upper Midwest: Mulberry >

Red-sided garter snake

The Red-sided garter snake is widely distributed across North America, ranging further north than any other species of snake, where it over-winters in underground dens by the tens of thousands. In spring, the males emerge first, surrounding the females as they appear. The snakes form a writhing mass of up to a hundred, sometimes rolling over the ground in "mating balls," till the female finally chooses a single male with which to mate.

In the Canadian province of Manitoba, many people gather in May to witness the emerging of the snakes. People are not the only ones waiting—hungry birds kill snakes by the hundreds. Garter snakes have no venom, and their only defense is to flee. Since they are cold-blooded, garter snakes are not able to move quickly when they first emerge, so some of the smaller males, apparently in order to protect themselves, imitate females by emitting a female pheromone. The other males then surround and protect them until their own body temperature has been elevated enough that they can escape the birds.

< 110 >

Wild hyacinth

Wild hyacinth, and other *Camassia* species, are generally edible, and were an important food source for many Indian tribes. The baked bulbs were similar to sweet potatoes, and when dried, could be pounded into flour.

The Nez Perce Indians offered sweet bread made from Camas root, and other native foods, to starving members of the Lewis and Clark Expedition in 1805. In his notes on their travels, Meriwether Lewis wrote appreciatively of the "sea of blue" of Camas plants and the Nez Perce's methods of preparing them.

Giant stag beetle

The male Giant stag horn beetle has antlerlike jaws that can be as long as its head and thorax combined. Like a deer, it uses them to do battle with other males during the breeding season. The stag beetle attempts to control a particular dead tree or stump, which the females use for egg laying. He may mate with several females.

Stag beetles only feed on dead wood, either fallen or standing. These places provide a sustenance-rich environment for larvae during their one to three year period of

< Secret Voices from the Forest - Volume II >

development. When large enough, they pupate for several months, emerging as adults, ready to start the breeding cycle again.

In spite of the impressive size of their jaws, stag beetles are unable to chew, and they only live for a few weeks as adults.

Ohio Spiderwort

Spiderwort flowers have a very short life—only a single morning—but each plant will produce twenty or more flowers per stem. It is often found in road-side ditches, and areas along railroads. Ohio Spiderwort is more resistant to the application of herbicides along railroads than most plants, which is one reason why it remains common in such areas.

Canada Goose

One of the heralds of spring and autumn is the sight of a large flock of Canada Geese flying overhead in a long, v-shaped formation. This technique, as well as flying with the wind, conserves energy and allows the flock to cover nearly 1,500 miles in a day. Because the bird in the front requires the most stamina, the lead position in the flight "wedge" is rotated. The usual altitude for the migratory flock is about 3,000 feet, although they have been seen as high as 29,000 feet.

< 111 >

Canada Geese populations have grown in recent times, partially due to the enactment of protective laws, but more because their natural predators have been removed or eliminated, and the birds have adapted to the altered terrain that has come with expanded urban development. The manicured lawns and man-made lakes and ponds of modern urbanization have also spread across the continent, helping the Canada Goose to become the most common waterfowl species in North America.

Because the Canada Goose adapts easily to human environments, non-migratory populations are on the rise. A twenty-one year study in Wichita, Kansas, completed in 2004, found the number of geese increase from 1,600 to 18,000 birds. Plentiful food and few enemies encourages the birds to remain in one location, contrary to their normal habits. Migration is taught to young birds, so if the parents do not fly south for the winter, their offspring will never learn the behavior.

< The Upper Midwest: Mulberry >

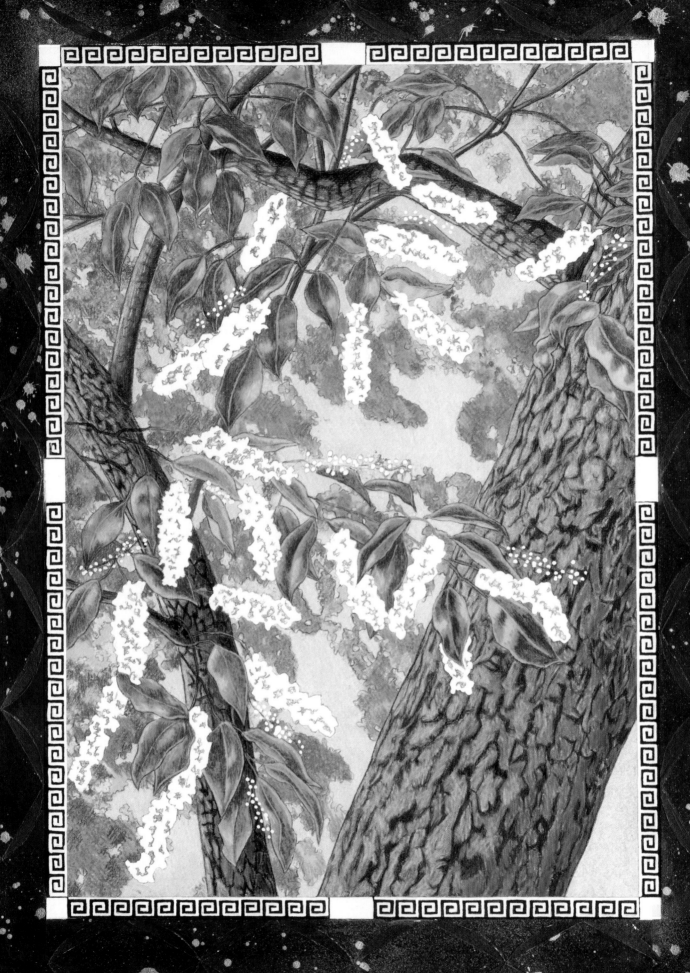

≼ BLACK CHERRY ≽

REFLECTIONS ON CAUSALITY

What Black Cherry Can Tell You About Itself

The Cycle of Life is like a great round—we feed others, who then grow, reproduce, die, and in time, feed the Earth, which feeds us in return. To this end, I make myself ripe and succulent, inviting you to consume. My sensuality is the force that makes life universally dynamic. I am merely a tiny example of this. All things have a purpose, and in order to survive, must find something to attract, and *be* attractive for—one thing is in hand with the other. This is the basic nature of *Causality*.

I can recall my time of dormancy, as a seed in the ground, waiting for the impulse to grow. It was a bit like dreaming—peaceful. Peace is lovely, as long as you have no desire; but when the impulse comes, it is irresistible. When that time comes, I love the warmth of spring, and the quickening. Then I may want to converse with other trees about the bees. We share the knowledge that the pollinators are nearby, so we can prepare ourselves for their visit. Though it is gratifying to be attractive to all, it is more productive to practice a selective strategy.

When I dream now, I am moving through the forest, visiting my friends, or perhaps experiencing another location. As a species, we encounter many environments, adding these places and conditions to our group awareness. I have chosen to live in the Upper Midwest because I feel a sense of the possibilities of "tomorrow." I find myself looking to the West.

From observation, I know that the practicalities of everyday life are profound, though they seem mundane. Without the continuous performance of simple acts, whether those that you choose consciously, or the ones your body seems to carry out of its own volition, life would soon cease to exist. Your lungs move air in and out of your body without the aid of thought. Could you go on very long if these actions were not accomplished? If you make the choice to stop eating and drinking, although it will take longer, life stops. Interaction with other forms of life is also vital. Though your body may survive isolation, your spirit will suffer. You become a non-functional entity, only important if and when your body becomes food for others.

Black Cherry's Place in the World

We are of the large and varied Rose Family, whose role is to sustain. Collectively, we feed everyone. There have been many that have emerged from the Progenitor, as new and different thought forms wished to become manifest. It could easily have been competitive, but the emergence of all those new species just seemed to prove that Possibility is without limits.

My own species, whose role here is as a facilitator, associated itself with certain emerging birds and insects, as they developed, long ago. We bring together, not just plants and animals, but also draw humans into the mix. Once only animals spread our seed, but your species has taken their place, and are no more or less arbitrary in your positioning of that seed.

In relation to that, one of the biggest changes we have seen to the planet is hybridization. Your species has done what Nature would possibly have done, and more. You do not consider consequences, but then, neither does Nature—it just absorbs them.

At the core of each thing, animate or inanimate, is a group of geometric configurations that determine the precise form—a formula, if you will. They themselves are conscious, living forms that reproduce and die, as their conglomerate, larger manifestations do. Sometimes they engage in the process of alteration, partially to function in a new way that will allow them to achieve a new purpose or action, and partially to entertain themselves. We see their forms reflected in the air itself.

Black Cherry's Message for Us

< 114 >

You cannot help but engage in the Cycle of Life, as it is an inevitable and inexorable process; but the peace that self-awareness and understanding brings has the power to change the future. Humanity's natural abilities give it the capacity to be an instrument of change on a grand scale, such as that of great herds of animals, or geological events. Believe it or not, embracing your animal nature, and accepting that you *are* a part of the animal creation, will allow you to follow your instincts without conflict. Because you have not done so for so long, you have misunderstood what that implies, interpreting it as license to behave without conscience, which is not at all the case.

When you align with a concept or a leader who has self-awareness and foresight, you alter the movement of astral energy which, in turn, changes the direction of fate. Learn to trust that the Universe, though inconceivably powerful and violent, is also seeking self-awareness, which will, by definition, have an enlightening outcome, at the very least. If you do not concentrate on discord and recrimination, you will find your intentions and actions will become more compassionate, and you will feel more in harmony with the cosmic design.

Become as intangible as smoke. It sounds impossible, but your minds have the capacity to comprehend the *physical* reality of the incorporeal body.

< Secret Voices from the Forest - Volume II >

CHRONICLES

< 115 >

The Black cherry, a member of the extensive Rose, or *Rosaceae* family, is a forest tree that needs a lot of sunlight, so it is quick to move into burned or otherwise damaged areas. The roots sprout extensively, and many seedlings result from fallen fruit. Sheltered from wind and diseases, it can become relatively large, at over one hundred feet, and live as long as two hundred years.

Prunus serotina means, "late plum." Its long bunches of tiny white flowers appear after the leaves develop, unlike other native cherries that bloom before the leaf growth has begun.

< The Upper Midwest: Black Cherry >

The seeds of the small, red and black fruits are spread in the droppings of birds and other wildlife, giving rise to new trees farther from the parent plant.

Black cherries are small and bitter tasting, so have little commercial value, but have long been used for food and medicine. Black cherry leaves and seeds, carbon-dated to between 4,500 and 5000 years ago, were found in Hinds Cave, a Paleolithic-era rock shelter in southwestern Texas.

Today, as well as the usual jams and jellies, Black cherry fruits are used to flavor wines, liquors and sodas. *Prunus serotina* has been used to develop cultivars with larger, sweeter fruits that have an even wider use in cooking, baking and the making of ice cream.

The rich, reddish-brown wood of the Black cherry is highly favored for cabinetry. It is hard and strong, close-grained and easy to work. Popular with colonists, the tree was introduced into European gardens as an ornamental as early as the 1600s. Because of its habit of sprouting, and the fact that it puts out root toxins, it has crowded out many of their own native species, and is now considered invasive.

Excepting the fruit, all parts of *Prunus serotina* are highly toxic, and potentially lethal to humans and many domesticated animals, including ruminants, such as cattle and sheep. The leaves, twigs, and bark contain compounds, when crushed or damaged by frost, which are converted to hydrogen cyanide, or prussic acid.

As late as 1975, both wild black cherry and chokecherry were listed in the U.S. Pharmacopoeia as sedatives and cough suppressants. Eating Black cherries has been shown to be helpful in the treatment of gout, a painful condition wherein high levels of uric acid in the bloodstream form crystals in the joint of the big toe. Other conditions that can be aggravated by excessive uric acid are kidney stones, osteoarthritis and bone spurs, as well as high blood pressure and heart disease.

Born in Suffolk, England in 1892, the racehorse named Black Cherry, a

< 116 >

< Secret Voices from the Forest - Volume II >

brown mare with a fairly unimpressive history when it came to wins and losses, gave birth to many foals, nine of which eventually won forty-one races. She died in 1917. It is thought her influence would have been greater had not the Germans confiscated some of her offspring located in France during the First World War.

Although there are several species of wild cherry native to North America, none of them is commercially cultivated for human consumption. The fruit of Black cherry, Pin cherry, and Chokecherry are too small and bitter to be of great value. The types of cherries familiar to today's cherry-eater originated in Europe.

The first cherry orchard specializing in sweet cherries was planted in Oregon in 1847, where the Bing and Lambert varieties were developed; later the Rainier was bred in Washington State from the Bing and another variety. These three varieties make up ninety-five per cent of the sweet cherry production. Washington State produces the most—264,000 tons in 2012.

Tart cherries are a specialty of the orchards of Michigan; the Montmorency was an early variety that is still widely used in baking, juices and other confections. Michigan has approximately four million cherry trees, each tree producing 150-200 pounds of cherries. Michigan usually harvests about sixty percent of tart cherries produced yearly in the United States. Traverse City, Michigan holds the National Cherry Festival in July, and calls itself the "Cherry Capital of the World."

Another "festival" happens every year in Michigan—the "Cherry Pit Spit," recognized by the Book of World Records as an official competition. It is held at the beginning of the cherry harvest. The current record for the longest spit is 100 feet, 4 inches.

< 117 >

Mythological references to cherries vary worldwide. In Japan, cherries represent beauty, courtesy and modesty. The Chinese placed cherry branches and statues carved from cherry wood in front of their doors on New Year's to keep evil spirits away. The Greeks had a unique group of supernatural beings called *Dryades*, the nymphs of the trees and forests, some of whom were associated with one particular kind of tree. The nymphs of cherry trees were called *Kraneiai*. At the birth of one of these, a tree arose from the earth, to which the Dryad's life was tied. While it thrived, so did its resident nymph, but when it died, her existence ended as well.

< The Upper Midwest: Black Cherry >

BLACK CHERRY COMPANIONS

Scarlet Tanager
Chlorociboria Aeruginascens
Kentucky Coffeetree
Reticulitermes Flavipes—Termite
Beautiful Wood Nymph
Inland Rush
Mourning Cloak
Common Pipewort
Cedar Waxwing
Ditch Stonecrop
Grey Tree Frog
13-lined Ground Squirrel
Yellow Pond Lily
Balsam Fir
Blue-spotted Salamander
Fairy Slipper
American Beaver
Water Arum

The little naughty girls,
the gypsy vagabonds, are hanging
longstemmed cherry pairs
over their pretty ears, twisting
them about their fingers, stepping
high and dainty as ladies do
and laughing...

Poison in the long leaves,
in the twig, poison right down
in the rings, a wrapping of poison
in the sinuous bark...

Among the girls' hair, next to the pale skin
of their necks, the smooth dark jewels
of desire; what unsaid thing
do their hearts reach for...

O, but the blossom is beautiful; and then
if every flower fattened into fruit...

Fly away, Children! Spread out
   on glossy wings, black
      as a raven's, bearing
         each in your crammed beak
            the stone to come.

FACTS ABOUT SOME BLACK CHERRY COMPANIONS

Cedar Waxwing

More so than most birds, the Cedar Waxwing specializes in eating fruit. It can go for months eating nothing else. Traveling in flocks of 30 to 100 birds, it often appears where there is a good crop of berries. When all the fruit is gone, the birds move on. Occasionally, the Cedar Waxwing will become intoxicated if it consumes overripe berries that have started to ferment.

An introduced variety of honeysuckle contains pigments that have contributed to a color change on the bands of some birds tail feathers, turning them from yellow to orange. This phenomenon was not noted before 1950.

Inland rush

Seeds of the Inland rush number 2,800,000 per ounce. The *Juncus* species grow exclusively in wetlands, and are mainly perennials, with all flower parts growing in multiples of three.

Rushlight is a type of candle or miniature torch once used as a cheap source of artificial light. The rushlight was made by dipping the pithy center of a peeled rush into kitchen grease, letting the fat harden, then placing it into pinched holders called *nips*. A twelve-inch rushlight would burn for about fifteen minutes.

Gray tree frog

The Latin name, *Hyla versicolor*, describes this frog well as, like a chameleon, it may be varying shades of gray, green, or brown, or be nearly black. The small suction-discs on its toes are large and well developed, making it an excellent climber, so it is commonly heard calling from high in the treetops. It can also climb walls and glass and can be seen at night clinging to houses, in pursuit of insects attracted by lights.

Unlike many other frogs that hibernate by burying themselves in the mud of a pond over winter, the Gray tree frog instead produces an anti-freeze called glycerol, and is thereby able to hibernate on land.

The female Gray tree frog chooses a mate according to the length of his call. Sometimes another male will sit

< Secret Voices from the Forest - Volume II >

< 120 >

in front of a male making a louder call, in order to intercept the responding female and mate with her himself.

Green oak wood fungus

Although common in hardwood forests throughout the world, this tiny, inedible fungus' fruiting bodies are not often seen. However, the brilliantly green-stained wood it produces through a chemical reaction in trees, such as oak, ash, poplar and aspen, is easy to find. It was used by Italian Renaissance woodworkers to create beautifully colored inlays in furniture; and later by craftsmen in Tunbridge Wells, Kent, to produce highly detailed inlaid wood pictures, which were often set into the lids of boxes. Called "Tunbridge ware," today these antiques are very valuable.

American beaver

The American beaver is the world's second largest rodent, and only the capybara of South America is larger. Its body is well adapted to aquatic life, with webbed hind feet for swimming, and has ears and nose with valve-like flaps that close underwater. There is also a *nictating* membrane, or extra eyelid, that protects the eyes, and lips that seal behind its large front incisors, allowing it to gnaw wood underwater.

< 121 >

Chewing through tree bark wears these front teeth down, but they continue to grow throughout the beaver's life, and are protected by tough, orange-colored enamel.

The largely nocturnal beaver is an herbivore, feeding on leaves, twigs, tree bark and roots, and other plants, like pond lilies and grasses. It is most closely related to rabbits and hares.

A beaver lodge is a dome-shaped structure made of tree trunks and branches of various sizes, woven together with grass, and plastered with mud. Using the same materials to build a dam, the beaver turns a slow-flowing stream into a deep pond, thereby protecting the underwater entrances to its lodge.

All those branches and logs must come from somewhere nearby, so the ideal placement of the beaver's dam is near *successional* growth trees, such as aspen, willow and cottonwood. *Succession*, in ecological parlay, is a term coined by Henry David Thoreau, referring to the process by which members of a plant community create conditions that no longer favor them, but promote the growth of larger or more complex members. When beavers abandon their lodges and dams for one reason or another, aquatic plants take over the pond.

< The Upper Midwest: Black Cherry >

It fills with silt and mud, eventually allowing shrubs, grasses and flowers to grow, and a meadow becomes established. Shrubs give shade and protection to tree seedlings, which in turn take over the area, and the land becomes woodland.

Balsam fir

This medium-sized conifer yields a resin called Canada balsam which, when purified and filtered, is nearly transparent. It was traditionally used to glue optical lenses and make permanent microscopic slides, and can be used to repair scratches in car windshields.

When steam-inhaled, Balsam fir oil has healing and antiseptic qualities beneficial in treatment of sinus and lung congestion. It is also useful as an aid to sleep or to give up smoking. As an essential oil, it is reported to bring emotional balance and security.

Eastern subterranean termite

Reticulitermes flavipes forms subterranean colonies of several hundred to several million individuals. Members of the highly organized community consist of three castes: workers, soldiers, and reproductives. The largest number of colony members, the workers, are sterile, and do all the grunt work, but are capable of molting into other castes. Soldiers, who only make up 1-2% of the colony, are defenders of the colony. They cannot molt into anything else, and also cannot feed themselves, so are fed by the workers. The reproductives, those destined to start new colonies, make up the rest.

All castes look different. Workers are blind, wingless, and about one-eighth of an inch long. Soldiers are slightly larger, and have large mandibles that are used for defense. *Alates* (future reproductives) have wings and compound eyes and are a darker color. Queens can produce up to 2000 eggs a day, developing extra sets of ovaries, so their bodies can become massive, their extended abdomens getting as long as 3.5 inches over the period of their forty-five year life spans. The king, who looks more like a worker, remains neces-sary to the queen's reproductive ability for life, unlike ant consorts, who mate with their queen only once, and then become superfluous.

Although termites ingest wood, they cannot digest wood fibers. They rely on protozoa, single-celled animals, and bacteria living in their gut to free up the cellulose.

Because termites can produce up to two liters of hydrogen from digesting a single sheet of paper, they are one of the planet's most efficient bioreactors. Fermenting bacteria in the bodies of the ter-mites produce simple sugars, which are then used again by other bacteria, producing hydrogen as a by-product. The U.S. Department of Energy is studying this process, and hopes there is potential to scale

< 122 >

< Secret Voices from the Forest - Volume II >

it up enough to generate commercial quantities of hydrogen from woody biomass.

Common pipewort

In bloom, these tiny, white flowers can be seen rising above the surface of shallow waters. *Eriocaulon aquaticum*, meaning "wooly stem," is an aquatic plant, with leaves and roots completely submerged. In Ayurvedic medicine, pipewort is used to treat fever and inflammation, jaundice and urinary tract diseases.

Mourning Cloak

These large, distinctive-looking butterflies, native to North America and Eurasia, are known for their longevity—up to a year. They tolerate cold well, so do not migrate. Instead, they hibernate in places which will receive direct sunlight, so their dark-colored wings will absorb as much heat as possible. Overwintering allows them to begin mating early. As the heat of summer becomes oppressive, they enter a state of estivation, or dormancy, in which they remain until fall, when they begin to feed again in preparation for hibernation.

The Mourning Cloak has a number of defense-mechanisms. It tends to rest on dark tree bark, where it can find camouflage, and when threatened by attack from birds or other butterflies, may join together with other of its species and make a menacing charge. It also makes loud clicks when flying away from a resting spot.

< 123 >

Yellow pond lily

This water lily is a perennial, growing in lakes, ponds and slow-moving rivers. Its bright yellow flowers contain many seeds which are eaten by a variety of waterfowl. Its large, round leaves are food and shelter for deer, beaver and muskrats, fish, amphibians and invertebrates. Its roots, or rhizomes, were used as food and medicine by many American Indian tribes.

The Menominee Indians of Wisconsin thought the plant, with its six-foot long stems, was an "Underneath Spirit," a source of "great medicine" and of fog on the lakes.

< The Upper Midwest: Black Cherry >

DO ALIENS EXIST? WHO CARES?

It's not that I absolutely won't buy that aliens have visited Earth, or that there are people who have been abducted. There are artifacts and legends from many ancient civilizations that seem to indicate guidance, bestowal of knowledge, and assistance (and/or interference) from greatly advanced beings that descended from the sky.

Some of the mysterious artifacts from the Sumerians, Aztecs and Mayans, Egyptians and others date back as far as 10,000 B.C.E., so I would certainly never say it's impossible. Hey, I loved the *X-Files* and *Star Trek: The Next Generation*, and one of my favorite old movies is *Hangar 18*, starring Darren McGavin, in which a really plausible theory was presented. The gist was:

• First, aliens checked out Planet Earth (at a somewhat indeterminate time in the past), and thought it was a fun place, and

• As an experiment, they engaged in some genetic engineering with the species of animal closest to themselves, which were ape-like creatures—don't laugh; I'll bet if somebody ever figures out the science, it'll only be a matter of time.

• After that, said experiment simmers for millions of years (talk about slow cooking) and Voila! Human Beings! It's a good movie, so for those who haven't seen it, I won't spoil it by revealing the end.

But here's my problem. If they're so advanced, and have been observed on Earth for literally thousands of years, what exactly do they want? What are they waiting for? I can't believe we're that entertaining. But if they want our natural resources, they'd better get a move on, before we use them all up. On the other hand, if they consider *us* the resource, and are in cahoots with the food industry to get us fattened up, I'd say the population of the U.S. might be just about ready for harvest. Well, at least I am.

I mean, let's be honest. The only purely investigative, altruistic explorers I've ever heard of were the crew of the starship *Enterprise*. Everybody else wants something that will, in some way or another, enhance their lives, whether it's for profit or survival. That would certainly apply to most human explorations. Even if the earthbound (or sea-bound) explorers of the last several centuries were themselves simply curious, most of the time they were funded by someone who figured *they'd* make a lot of money. Am I right?

So why would aliens be any different?

< 124 >

< Secret Voices from the Forest - Volume II >

All this is debatable, of course, but my real point is: forget about looking for aliens in outer space. We've been surrounded by alien life forms since we crawled out of the mud—all the rest of the animals *and all of the plants*. We've never been able to communicate with them through language, so we assume they are less intelligent or, in the case of plants, not even sentient.

I think that's presumptuous. No one knows how many life forms exist on this planet, but we have a pretty good idea (in really round numbers) of how long most things have been around. Bacteria and algae appeared about 2 billion years ago, land plants began developing 430 million years ago, reptiles approximately 300 million, and land mammals around 75 million years ago. Not to mention, everything works together and depends on everything else. So what gives us the idea all these life forms don't have ways of communicating? Just because *we* don't have the capacity to understand their processes doesn't mean that nothing's going on in there.

Modern man has only been around for about 300,000 years—new kid on the block. And, like children, we believe that everything revolves around us. It's an understandable position—for children. But for grownups, it seems to me to be an absurd, egocentric concept that is just about ready for retirement—at least, if we plan on being able to live on this planet in comfort much longer.

In *The Outermost House*, Henry Beston said, "In a world older and more complete than ours [animals] move finished and complete, gifted with extensions of the senses we have lost or never attained, living by voices we shall never hear."

I believe this applies to plants as well.

Whether aliens are currently abducting humans (and/or cows), upon which to perform experiments, or are monitoring our behavior, I don't see that it makes any difference to how we as humans should behave. At the moment, we spend the vast percentage of our time, money and resources beating up on each other—or at least that's what the guys running things seem to be doing. The rest of us are saying either, "Ain't it awful," like me, or "I just want to get on with my life." Well, come to think of it, that's me, too.

This is my rationale for being a self-proclaimed "Treetalker." I mean, why not? They've been around a long time, and must see and know a whole lot more than we do and, to quote a well known, but not entirely respected "news" paper, "I want to know!"

< 125 >

< The Upper Midwest >

CHAPTER FOUR

THE LOWER MIDWEST

myriad life-streams
seep silently through the land
becoming oceans

≫≫≫≫≫≫≫≪≪≪≪≪≪≪

THE LOWER MIDWEST

Like the Upper Midwest, this is an erratically defined area. The U.S. Census Bureau thinks it's one thing, while the National Weather Service thinks it's another, and the U.S. Geological Society has *two different* definitions, so I feel justified in picking and choosing what suits me. Generally, I am referring to an area that is "moderate in all things"—in heat, cold, precipitation, terrain (no high mountains, or flat-as-far-as-you-can-see prairies), and it is moderate, as well, in more human concerns, such as economics, politics and religion, although those issues are not topics covered here.

In many ways, this area is similar to the Upper Midwest. It is predominantly farm and ranch land, small towns and rural communities, with a handful of large cities, each having populations ranging from 200,000 to 3 million. One noticeable characteristic of Midwestern cities is that they build *out*, rather than *up*, since they have room.

< 128 >

But this was not always the case. Long before the Europeans discovered this continent, humans had been crossing the Bering Strait into North America from Asia—for perhaps 30,000 years, following herds of animals (who were apparently after all that grass!). It is generally thought that Asia-to-America Paleo-migration had finished by 12,000 B.C.E. Then, to make a long, *long* story short, they spread out over the continent, forming family/tribal units, and in some cases, quite large urban groups. These communities were characterized by large earthworks, used for not only burials but, like those in Mexico and South America, for ceremonial and religious purposes, including allowing the Sun God's earthly representative closer proximity to the Divine Source.

These early, indigenous cultures have been collectively called "Mound Builders," after the typical practice of creating platform pyramids or mounds, cones, concentric ridges or other forms, by moving great quantities of earth. They seemed to have generally gravitated to the Gulf Coast and the Mississippi River and its tributaries, as these were reliable sources of food from fishing and hunting, as well as agriculture, as maize was widely grown in the rich land of the floodplain. The rivers were also ideal for travel and trade.

These mounds pre-date the building of the pyramids in Egypt by 1000 years. The earliest known archaeological site, named "Watson Brake," dates from 5400 years ago. Over the many centuries, there were many different groups that built, occupied, and abandoned these locations, the next community adding more structures. Usually the settlement was a complex of earthworks, and was sometimes populated by many thousands of people.

Current opinion has it that monument building is one of the first signs of advanced civilization, as it brings large groups of people together, working for a unified purpose. Archaeo-

< Secret Voices from the Forest - Volume II >

logical records show that the early American Indian cultures not only made pottery and worked in stone, but also with metal, and inscribed their handiwork with symbols that could have been an early writing system, also products of larger, unified community.

Europeans made record of contact with them as early as the mid-16th century, when there were still many large, well-populated villages and towns; but, only a few decades later, the villages were empty and the mounds abandoned. The most probable scenario is that the inhabitants had died from diseases for which they had no defense, and new mound building ceased around that time. Although no longer permanently occupied, some of these sites still exist, and a few have been protected as National Heritage Sites. They are still used as places of worship by certain American Indian tribes, although many others have been looted, vandalized, or otherwise destroyed by farming or development.

Another interesting aspect of this area is the New Madrid Seismic Zone, halfway between St. Louis and Memphis, which was the site of four earthquakes that occurred within a three-month period over the winter of 1811/1812, each estimated at 8.0 on the Richter scale. Since there were barely any residents in the region at the time, this event doesn't have a place in our national history equivalent to the great San Francisco earthquake of 1906, which reached a magnitude of 7.8. The resulting fires from that quake destroyed 80% of the city, whose population was, at that time, about 400,000.

The 1811-12 New Madrid earthquakes created a lake in Tennessee, sent shocks that could be felt as far away as Boston and Washington, D.C., caused 18 ½ square miles of earth to liquefy around the small town of Little Prairie, and temporarily reversed the flow of the Mississippi River.

Precisely underneath the site of the original New Madrid, Missouri town, is another of the "failed faults," formed millions of years ago, when the youthful (in geologic time) continent of Laurentia was reacting to yet another collision, coming from the north, by attempting to separate itself from earlier continental incorporations.

This seismic zone is still active, although it's been over a hundred years since an earthquake of relatively large magnitude has occurred—but the U.S. Geological Society isn't ruling out future quakes.

⪻ PECAN ⪼

REFLECTIONS on STEADFASTNESS

What Pecan Can Tell You About Itself

By being a sure source of food and shelter, I create a bulwark, a check against the inevitable challenges of life that face those who surround me. Then I am *Steadfastness*, manifesting a powerful urge to love and care for all, including myself. You can also see this in mothers of all species, in the care and security they give to their offspring, and generally in anything that shows an instinct for helping those that are weaker or enduring difficult circumstances.

I would like to still be around when the next great change comes. Yes, that concerns evolution, insofar as evolution itself is the response of physicality to an underlying transformation taking place in the *totality*. It is well known that this next phase is already underway, but on an imperceptible level. The change will be so subtle that you may not notice, or if you do, even believe what you see.

There is the possibility that a reshaping of this magnitude will take many thousands of years . . . or not. The future has no boundaries, and yet lives completely within the confines of hope, fear, anticipation or surprise, and is dependent on the measure of their interaction.

This movement is an interactive response — your cells make a decision, then others answer, then cells outside of you react, and on and on. The need for continuation will create the desire to awaken from a repose that seems to have been established shortly after the last Ice Age.

I have taken up residence in the Lower Midwest, because I prefer the warmth and humidity. Also, there is a dreamlike quality to the days that allows the mind to wander freely. When I dream, or drift, I see past the beautiful, impressive, or remarkable physical aspects of my surroundings, to the momentous fact that each thing exists in the *first* place. I reflect on why each form has chosen itself, or been chosen, whichever is the case. Perhaps they are the same, as we are all parts of the whole.

Pecan's Place in the World

We calm fears, thereby bringing peace, at least temporarily, through plenty. We, too, are members of the Walnut family, which all provide food and shelter without discrimination. We are the most elegant, most refined of the family. It comes from being imaginative with our responses and from allowing our thoughts to range freely.

The Pecan tree has learned a few things that may seem obvious (but that is why they are taken for granted), such as: Earth likes the color green; the planet often hiccups, or even passes gas (it is not self-conscious)—although you may experience these as earthquakes and volcanoes; Earth has no reality on cessation of existence, which it has passed on to all its inhabitants.

Pecan's Message for Us

In you, Steadfastness is in evidence during times of challenge—not simply the problems that arise as a result of catastrophic events, but in the ennui that may come while performing daily tasks, which may offer no particular interest or enjoyment, but need attention regardless. Seeing to immediate needs does tend to remove, or at least temporarily push aside, the attention you put on the past and the future. Both the past and the future have their attending host of hopes and fears, and your need to record your own passing simply compounds the situation.

You have created these concepts of the passage of time, which have their relevance, of course. They help you manage and structure your *own* trial and error results. However, be mindful that they can detract from living to the fullest extent possible in each moment and, if read only literally, may limit the direction of your evolution.

In order to raise the level of your group consciousness further, you must recognize that physical bodies, physical endeavors, physical functions, the entire physicality of existence, is not something lesser, or irrelevant, or a horror, even amidst the brutality of its life-and-death struggles. It is an awe-inspiring process of trial and error in which we all have no choice but to engage. The only way through is by being aware, and offering compassion to every creature, not least of all to humanity.

< 132 >

< Secret Voices from the Forest - Volume II >

CHRONICLES

< 133 >

Native to the United States and Mexico, the Pecan is a large, long-lived tree, related to hickories and walnuts. The Spanish explorers, observing that the pecan was a staple foodstuff for American Indians, quickly realized its value. During the 16th century, they introduced the tree into Europe, Asia and Africa. Though it is now widely grown, the pecan only became commercially significant in the 1880s.

Today, the United States produces the lion's share of the world's crop from more than ten million trees, with an annual crop of 150-200 thousand tons of nuts. There are over five hundred cultivars of the Pecan tree that have been developed in the United States. Albany, Georgia, with over 600,000 pecan trees is called the "Pecan capital of the United States," and

< The Lower Midwest: Pecan >

several pecan-producing states hold yearly pecan festivals. But the State of Texas designated the pecan as their official state tree in 1919, and produces more nuts from the native pecan species than anywhere else in the world.

A pecan tree does not begin to bear fruit for approximately ten years, but can go on producing nuts for up to 300 years. Pecan nuts are not picked. When the fruit is ripe, the outer husk, or shuck, opens, allowing the inner nut to fall to the ground. The nuts are not edible until that time, so there is a considerable amount of competition from squirrels, who are able to pick the nuts off the tree before they are ready to drop.

The pecan, like many nuts, is a powerhouse of health benefits. A rich source of protein, they also contain high levels of omega-6 fatty acids and plant sterols, which aid in reducing LDL cholesterol. Research found that eating a small number of pecans each day may help in lowering cholesterol levels as efficiently as some prescription medications. A handful of pecans will also provide about ten percent of the daily requirement of zinc.

It would be impossible to discuss pecans without mentioning pecan pie. Every southern cook has a favorite recipe, and there seems to be as many "Old-fashioned," and "authentic" recipes for pecan pie as there are cooks. Several predecessors, such as the treacle, or molasses pie, which has been around since the Middle Ages, and sugar pies, chess pies, transparent pies, maple syrup and caramel pies, are all variations on a theme. Many have searched for a true pecan pie recipe from the 1800s, but food historians mainly agree that this rich dessert is a creation of the 20th century. There have been several claims, but no written record can be produced. The well-known cookbooks, such as *Fannie Farmer* and *Joy of Cooking*, do not feature pecan pie recipes until after 1940.

The invention of corn syrup, in 1882, provided a new liquid sweetener, and most "classic" recipes are a mixture of eggs, sugar, corn syrup and pecans, plus a little butter and vanilla for added flavor—or, if one feels risqué, chocolate or bourbon whisky.

< 134 >

< Secret Voices from the Forest - Volume II >

Speaking of molasses, you wouldn't normally think of a sweetening agent as an instrument of catastrophe, would you? In the early 20th century, molasses was one of the most popular sweeteners. Also, in combination with grain alcohol, it created ethanol, which was used to produce cordite, which was classified as an explosive. It is thought that munitions manufacturers, who had prospered during World War I, were looking for new sources of income, and planned to use their stocks of molasses to cash in on the pre-prohibition rush to buy alcohol, another product in which molasses played a sizeable part.

In December of 1915, U.S. Industrial Alcohol constructed a large storage tank near to the Boston harbor, where ships arrived from Cuba, bearing the basic product, and near the railway, convenient for shipment to factories. It was a densely populated area, with immigrant housing, blacksmith shops, a slaughterhouse, and the trolley company's freight sheds. The fifty-foot high tank had been hurriedly built, the construction overseen by a financial officer with no engineering experience. He could not read the plans and sought no advice. Upon completion, the tank should have been tested for strength by filling it with water, but as a delivery of molasses was due, the test was never made. From the very beginning, there were leaks. Local residents regularly scraped the leaking molasses into containers for home use, while rumbling noises emitted from the structure. The tank's owner responded to warnings of structural problems by painting the tank brown.

< 135 >

On January 15, 1919, after several days of freezing and thawing temperatures, the tank burst, sending a 2.2 million gallon tsunami of molasses, weighing 26 million pounds, out into the neighborhood. The huge wave, traveling at 35 mph, destroyed everything in its path, including the elevated train tracks. It was weeks before all the bodies were found. The cleanup took some 87,000 man-hours, and the harbor water was brown for a month.

The resulting legal case was the longest in Boston's history. The judge, finding the company liable, took six years to reach his verdict, recommending about $300,000 in damages, equivalent to several million today. Significantly, from that time on, Boston city authorities began requiring any plans for construction projects be signed off by an engineer or architect and filed with the city's building department. This practice soon spread throughout America.

< The Lower Midwest: Pecan >

PECAN COMPANIONS

Scarlet and Blue Leafhopper
Virgin's Bower
Clammy Ground Cherry
Devil Crayfish
Dictyophora Duplicata
Red Satyr
Indian Pink
Lesser Prairie Chicken
Sideoats Gramma Grass
Texas Sophora
9-banded Armadillo
Bronze Frog
Scarlet Gilia
Red Paper Wasp
Hackberry
Texas Mouse
Spurred Butterfly Pea
Wood Duck

Ah, you beauties;
you green the tallest airs
with your lush grace.
You look out and see rivers
spreading across the plain,
but neither rolling thunders, nor low flashes,
nor high winds from the South
can shake you —until
at the proper hour...

the smooth nuts fall,
dropping into long grass like rain
in a slow summer storm.

FACTS ABOUT SOME PECAN COMPANIONS

Nine-banded armadillo

Although there are twenty different species of armadillo, only one is native to North America. *Armadillo* is a Spanish word that means "little armored one," referring to the bony plates that cover most of this animal's body. It is the only living mammal that wears this kind of shell. The Nine-banded armadillo is closely related to the anteater and the sloth, but can move quite quickly when it is disturbed. Unlike other species of armadillo, this species is unable to roll into a ball.

Only active during warm periods, an armadillo has a low metabolism and no fat stores, so it cannot tolerate cold. In spite of that, the Nine-banded armadillo continues to expand its range north, since it has so few predators. It spends the majority of its time in one of its many burrows, which it digs with strong front claws.

Because of the weight of its shell relative to its body, when crossing a shallow stream, an armadillo can hold its breathe and walk across the bottom, but if the body of water is deeper, the animal will ingest air to inflate its stomach and intestines, thereby allowing it to become buoyant enough to float across.

Indian pink

Other common names for this native wildflower include Pinkroot and Wormgrass. It is popular with gardeners because it grows well in the shade, attracts hummingbirds, and has a long blooming period.

Practitioners of Flower Essence therapy believe that Indian pink helps those who have difficulty maintaining a sense of inner stability.

Traditionally, it was used by the Creek and Cherokee as a treatment for intestinal worms, and was collected and marketed to European traders. Because of its medicinal properties, it was over-harvested during the early 19th century but, as with any natural remedy not well understood, it is likely to have been administered carelessly, and some patients died from the treatment. By the mid-1800's, the dangers seem to outweigh the benefits, and medicinal use of the plant was largely discontinued. Because of this respite, Indian pink has made a comeback, and is again gracing wildflower gardens.

Lesser Prairie Chicken

The Lesser Prairie Chicken nests in oak, grass and sage prairies of five states in the southern plains, and is well known for its extravagant courtship dances. Once widely distributed, its population is at less than 10% of its pre-European settlement numbers. The Natural Resources Conservation Service, working with several state and private agencies, is offering incentives to ranchers and farmers to improve habitat for threatened and endangered species of plants and animals such as the Lesser Prairie Chicken.

Many of the proposed practices, such as prescribed burning, brush management, and restoration and management of rare or declining habitats, also promote healthy grazing lands for livestock.

Clammy ground cherry

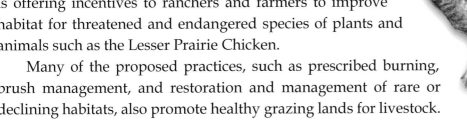

To bees and other insects, the Clammy ground cherry is a source of pollen and nectar, but its leaves and unripe fruit are toxic to humans and other mammals, because it contains high level of an alkaloid poison called *solanine*, which has fungicidal and pesticidal properties, and is part of the plant's natural defenses.

Clammy ground cherry is a member of the Nightshade family, along with nearly 3000 other species, including tomatoes, potatoes and eggplant. These familiar vegetables also contain solanine, and there are many in the health community who believe these foods can cause an allergic reaction, in those who are susceptible, that can lead to joint damage and arthritis.

On the other hand, some extracted compounds have been used to treat asthma, heart conditions and urinary disorders, and there is currently investigation into its potential to treat tumors.

< 139 >

Devil crayfish

With an appearance similar to a miniature lobster, the Devil crayfish is related to crabs and shrimps. The scientific designation is *Cambarus diogenes*, taking the name of the Greek philosopher, Diogenes, who is said to have lived outside in a round tub in order to demonstrate poverty as a virtue.

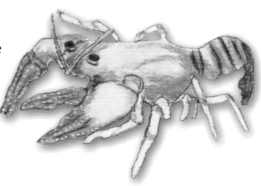

< The Lower Midwest: Pecan >

Virgin's bower

Virgin's bower is a member of the Buttercup family, and while attractive to hummingbirds and butterflies, it is toxic to nearly everything else. This plant may have been used as one possible ingredient in what was called by European colonists, "the Black Drink," a brew prepared by several southeastern American Indian tribes. It was named for its dark brown or black color.

The black drink was a traditional beverage prepared by special village officials as a purifier that could remove spiritual and physical contamination from the drinker. Its consumption was often followed by ritual vomiting, that heightened the drink's purgative and purifying powers by expelling contamination from the body. It was never taken on a casual basis, its use restricted to before and during important council meetings, celebratory dances, and the Green Corn and other ceremonies.

Wood Duck

< 140 >

The Wood Duck is considered one of the most beautiful species of wild fowl in North America. Males are an iridescent chestnut and green, with ornate patterns on nearly every feather.

It makes its nest in holes in trees in wooded swamps. Unlike the webbed feet of most ducks, the Wood Duck has strong claws for gripping bark and tree branches. However, it does not make its own cavities, and nest boxes will be readily used. The nest is made as close to water as possible. After hatching, the mother calls to her ducklings, which jump to the ground without injury, sometimes from heights as great as 290 feet.

Stinkhorn

Stinkhorns are repellent to us, but, covered with a slime that is reported to smell like rotting meat, they draw flies and ants, which spread the fungus' spores. Attracting insects to implement pollination is the same form of reproduction used by flowering plants. It is evolutionarily a more recent method, and considered more advanced by Botanists.

Bronze frog

The mating call of the Bronze frog is usually a single

< Secret Voices from the Forest - Volume II >

twang that sounds like someone plucking a loose banjo string, giving the frog the common name of "banjo frog."

Scarlet gilia

The flower of the Scarlet gilia is trumpet-shaped, with a long narrow tube that is designed for long-beaked or tongued pollinators, such as hummingbirds and moths.

This plant is widely distributed, with flower colors ranging from red to shades of pink to white. Sometimes flower petals change color throughout the course of a season, blooming red, timed to attract particular hummingbirds as they migrate, then turning white to attract moths, which will continue to pollinate their flowers until the end of the blooming season.

Red Paper Wasp

Paper wasps gather fibers from dead wood and plant stems, mix them with saliva, and construct water-resistant nests from the resulting papery material. The nests have open combs with cells for brood rearing, with a stalk that anchors the nest in a sheltered area. Although they are very territorial, paper wasps will generally only attack if they or their nests are threatened.

< 141 >

Since they are attracted to flowery smells, sugary substances, and the colors white and yellow, it is wise to avoid these things at a picnic. One clever way to keep wasps away at your get-together is to hang a paper bag close by, shaped roughly like a wasp nest, so they will think there is a rival wasp colony in the area and avoid it.

Recent research has found that paper wasps have face recognition abilities comparable to humans. "Faces are extremely important to species such as humans," said the study coauthor Michael Sheehan, a Ph.D. candidate at the University of Michigan in Ann Arbor.

"Studies show that when you look at a face, your brain treats it in a totally different way than it does other images," he said. "It's just the way the brain processes the image of a face, and it turns out that these paper wasps do the same thing."

The species *Polistes fuscatus* is unique in that it has extremely variable facial patterns from member to member. The study suggests that the paper wasps' brains are tuned to recognize faces of their own species, which helps them discern enemies, or those ranking higher in the hierarchy, thereby maintaining social order.

The venom of paper wasps is highly toxic to predatory mammals like wolves and cats, as well as birds of prey. Scientists in Spain have recently shown that larger and more brightly colored wasps contain more toxin than others.

< The Lower Midwest: Pecan >

⋞ CATALPA ⋟

REFLECTIONS ON EXTRAVAGANCE

What Catalpa Can Tell You About Itself

You never pass by me without giving me your attention. I have *really* big leaves, *really* long seedpods, and beautiful, showy clusters of flowers. I am the embodiment of exuberance, embracing Life in its entirety. I am the personification of *Extravagance*, giving my all, spending all my energy at once. I love the movement that even a tiny breeze can generate in my foliage, as I am then able to visit many new places, spreading my seeds and my essence.

But I am not the only one who manifests extravagance. The weather system of this planet moves endlessly, like a cat chasing its tail, creating eddies and maelstroms alike, swirling, twisting, surging, as though it will be able to continue doing so forever. We Catalpa have learned that because of the age and volatility of the planet, countless other species of plant and animal have come and gone, with all traces of them having vanished forever. Our desire is to pass the knowledge of uncertainty on to those that follow us; so, being an example, we hold nothing back, having faith that more will be available when it is required. Do as we do—relish your time here—be extravagant!

Once there were huge animals that roamed these prairies, who loved to eat our seeds. They spread them far beyond the territory to which the wind would have carried them. These creatures are gone now, but because of them we have been able to see much more of this wonderful land, and to watch how it has changed. I know this, because I was one of them once—a Giant sloth. I learned that it was sometimes good to be the biggest thing around!

When I dream, I remember the past, when things in the world were bigger, and more lush. Most of us plants, and the animals, too, have reduced ourselves in size to accommodate the current climactic conditions. I *almost* remember being the memory of one of my ancestors. The thought-form eventually took on its own life and personality, as well as the desire to become something *just* a little different. The will to live can accomplish almost anything!

Catalpa's Place in the World

The land has moved, and continues to do so, advancing over great distances. You don't notice, because your comprehension of the speed at which time passes is a good deal more hurried than ours. This area, the Lower Midwest, was once cooler, but has been dry land for considerably longer than areas north of here. It follows that this land has more memory, and is therefore more secure in its identity, as wisdom comes with age and experience.

We are a formerly tropical species that migrated north. Our function is to keep conditions from getting too regimented and orderly. Mess is natural! Besides, is there not use for all matter, even bits that seem to be waste? Many creatures thrive on these discarded fragments, wasting nothing.

"Wealth" is another inaccurate word. I create the illusion of wealth by making myself bright and ostentatious. Let the Magpie in you take note—bright and shiny doesn't always equate with valuable, although it can make you *believe* the situation is not so bad!

Another way to consider refuse is as *detritus*—or the organic matter that once was living cells and tissues. As the spirits of many beings who have passed in and out of existence over the many long epochs, they are really still present, having become the dust from which new forms arise. Their collective wisdom has been retained and added to the memories and potential that makes up the future.

Catalpa's Message to Us

You have always understood the concept of extravagance, and prefer it to "hiding your light under a bushel," as the saying goes. More and more, you are proving that you are able to extend your appreciation of the flamboyant to others who inhabit the planet, just for its own sake, rather than needing to find an application of their gifts to your needs. This has come with the maturation of your species, and your ability to learn from your mistakes.

< 144 >

When you follow your desire for knowledge to move forward, which you will, observe the source of your enthusiasm and understand your motivations, and you will make wise decisions.

< Secret Voices from the Forest - Volume II >

CHRONICLES

< 145 >

In North America, there are five native species of flowering trees and vines from the primarily tropical Bignonia Family (sounds like Begonia, but isn't.) The largest member, the Northern catalpa, is hardy and adaptable, with clusters of showy white flowers and seedpods that look like string beans. Its relatives include several kinds of Trumpet and creeper vines, Cat's claw, Cape honeysuckle, Desert willow and Pau d'arco.

< The Lower Midwest: Catalpa >

The name "catalpa" was a misinterpretation of the Indian word "Catawba," the name of a Southeastern Indian Nation whose official headquarters are today near Rock Hill, South Carolina. The tree is their tribal totem, and is more commonly known as the Catawba in that area.

Catalpa is fast growing, but short-lived, to an average of sixty to seventy years, yet there are rare instances of it living to twice that age. Its prominent heart-shaped leaves can be a foot long and eight inches wide, and the seed pods up to two feet long, so the tree is very distinctive and can be easily recognized at a distance. The gently fragrant flowers are tempting, both to bees, during the daylight hours, and, because they are mostly white, to moths at night.

In the late 1800s, the Hunnewell brothers, who were both railroad men, established a 400-acre catalpa plantation near Farlington, Kansas, and set about promoting the use of catalpa for railroad ties, telephone poles, and fuel. They sold thousands of seeds to accompany an advertising pamphlet, which helped to spread the catalpa throughout the Great Plains and Midwest.

< 146 >

Steam-powered locomotives, run on commercial railways, were one of the inventions that helped the industrial revolution sweep the world. Wagonways or tramways, the early predecessors of railways, go back as far as 6th century B.C. Greece, when a limestone track with parallel grooves, called the *Diolkos*, was constructed to move boats and their goods across the Isthmus of Corinth, saving mariners a long and perilous journey. Later, in 16th century Germany, carts were pulled on wooden planks, with a guide pin between the planks to keep the carts on the track. This system was primarily used to move coal and metal ore. All metal, flanged wheels did not replace this system for 200 years. Steel replaced iron, the steam engine was invented, and economic motivation and the needs of war created enough focus to perfect the steam locomotive.

The British Empire was instrumental in establishing railway systems in Canada—by 1870, the Grand Trunk Railway was the longest in the world—as well as India and Pakistan, where extensive rail systems were constructed from 1840 to 1870, although their importance was not fully realized for many years afterwards. In Europe, Belgium, France and Germany led the way in stimulating industry and connecting cities with ports, mining areas and manufacturing hubs. Mexico had over 15,000 miles of track, which linked agricultural regions to seaports, but they were largely nationalized in 1909.

In the United States, the industrialized Northeast linked to the farms and ranches of the Midwest by 1860. The South concentrated on short lines, linking cotton regions to ports. The lack of interconnected rail lines severely hampered their efforts to get weapons and supplies to troops during the American Civil War. Following 1865, the rush to connect the coasts was on, and in Ogden, Utah, in 1869, the transcontinental railroad was completed, with the driving of a symbolic golden spike. Railways were the primary facilitators of national commerce until the construction of interstate highways, which began after World War II.

There are two distinct species of Catalpa in North America, the Northern and the Southern. The Southern, smaller and more shrub-like, is attacked by the Catalpa sphinx moth more frequently than the Northern species.

< Secret Voices from the Forest - Volume II >

Both species have naturalized far beyond their small native ranges. Their striking appearance, quick growth and ability to adjust to varying conditions have prompted homeowners to plant them as ornamentals. Before that, European settlers planted these trees to harvest them for fence posts, as they grew quickly, and the heartwood, when buried, is highly resistant to rot for several years.

The larvae of several aphids and other small insects, as well as certain moths, feed heavily on the leaves. Catalpa trees are the single host for the Catalpa sphinx moth, which, when numerous, can defoliate a tree entirely. In March and April, masses of eggs are laid on the underside of leaves, each clump containing from a hundred to a thousand eggs. After a few days, the caterpillars emerge, feeding as a group. Taking about three weeks to become full-grown, they move down the tree, enter the soil at the foot of the tree to pupate, and emerge in two weeks as adults. There can be as many as four generations each year, depending on location, with the last generation overwintering in the soil.

In an unusual defense strategy, the Catalpa has secondary *nectaries*, or nectar-producing glands, at the base of each leaf stem, which help to attract ants, ladybugs and wasps. They, in turn, feed on the caterpillars, aphids and mealybugs, generally keeping their numbers in check.

< 147 >

Some enterprising folks actually maintain plantations of catalpas, in order to produce caterpillars from the Catalpa sphinx moth, which are prized as fish bait by many Southern anglers. When well fed, the caterpillars are "juicy," with tough skins, and can be frozen for later use.

The idea that humans have extended the natural range of the catalpa is perhaps mistaken. In 1976, an archeological dig in West Virginia revealed *Catalpa speciosa* (Northern catalpa) to be present in that location around 1500 A.D., and fossil remains have been discovered in rocks of the Yellowstone River, in Montana, dating back to the Miocene era, which was a minimum of five million years ago.

The Catalpa's wood is soft and light, weighing only 26 pounds per cubic foot when dry, making it excellent for carving and boatbuilding. Catalpa is often used to reclaim land, such as areas that have been strip-mined, because it successfully grows where air pollution, poor drainage, compacted soil, and drought are difficulties for other species.

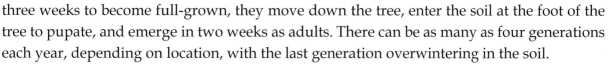

< The Lower Midwest: Catalpa >

CATALPA COMPANIONS

Osage Orange
American Robin
Alligator Snapping Turtle
Venus Looking Glass
Red Fox
Red Love Grass
Marbled Salamander
Texas Bluebonnet
Barn Owl
Hoary Puccoon
Redfin Pickerel
American Badger
Coltricia montagnei
Blue Cohosh
Miterwort
Sphinx Moth Caterpillar
Bee Balm

Where the spirit's large with a whole lot
to give, it's going to get out
somewhere. Maybe that's why
I stretch out such big leaves,
Flat as the skins on jungle drums;
and why I let my long seedpods hang down
voluptuously in the humid air
—and how about this for a flower!
   a spillage of jewels on a silken lap,
    pretty as an orchid— but I don't just give one,
I throw out thousands! A whole carnival of fancy blooms.
So let's everyone fling out all their colours
In a rosary-rain of gaudy beads: over marching bands
panting through narrow streets like slow gilded serpents;
at the passing float, swaying over the noisy crowd
like some loud, crazy, painted smile
—because didn't you know? The Gods are always
        delirious with delight. And don't you know?
            Heaven's laugh is the huge
                over-abundance of beauty on Earth.

FACTS ABOUT SOME CATALPA COMPANIONS

Red fox

The most widespread carnivore in the world, the Red fox is the largest species of the genus *Vulpes*, and is able to adapt quickly to new environments. The male does not form a pack, but rather has one or two mates, each with young, within his particular range.

The Red fox's most exceptional hunting ability is its hearing. It can hear crows flying one-third of a mile away, and a mouse squeak over three hundred feet away. It is an omnivore, consuming whatever is available, sometimes including a large quantity of fruit.

Red foxes have become well established in many large cities throughout the world, most commonly in residential suburbs. It is speculated by some researchers that the urban fox is developing into a different species, because it's diet is mainly man-made foods—with accompanying additives—and it has developed a different set of survival skills. As Dimitri Belyaev's 1953-64 research showed about the changes in foxes when domesticated, we now know it is possible the foxes will have developed strikingly new physical differences in just a few generations.

Osage orange

Although the Osage orange was once limited to an area including parts of Arkansas, Oklahoma and Texas, it is now a common sight on the Great Plains and other areas of the country, because of the practice of planting the relatively short, thorny tree in tight rows, where it would become a windbreak or nearly impenetrable living fence. With the invention of barbed wire in 1874, this practice was largely discontinued, but the trees remained and spread. It was then found that the tough tree's rot-proof and mostly insect-proof stems made fence posts that "could outlast the wire." The Osage Indians prized this strong wood for making bows.

The grapefruit-sized fruit is a magnet for any nearby squirrel. A near relative of the Mulberry, the tree's fruit bears a certain resemblance to unripe mulberries, but when ripe, has an orange-like scent. It also contains an anti-fungicide that deters insects, and many swear by the folk remedy of putting "hedge apples" in their house to keep out spiders and other insects.

Catalpa sphinx moth

A female Catalpa sphinx moth lays up to a thousand eggs on the leaves of a Catalpa tree in spring. When they hatch, the caterpillars work their way down the tree, molting several times. After two to three weeks, they reach the ground, where they pupate in the soil. Adults emerge a few days later and the cycle begins again. In warmer areas, there can be as many as five generations per year, all feeding exclusively on Catalpa leaves. Fortunately, defoliated Catalpas produce new leaves promptly.

Blue cohosh

Blue Cohosh, known also as Papoose Root or Squawroot, has been used for centuries as a herbal toner and remedy for many sorts of women's reproductive issues, as well as intestinal problems.

Alligator snapping turtle

The Snapping turtle of today is very similar to *Proganochelys*, its primitive ancestor of 215 million years ago, which predates dinosaurs by 100 million years. However, because of its spiked shell and beaklike jaws, the Alligator snapping turtle is often referred to as "the dinosaur of the turtle world." This species is confined to river systems that drain into the Gulf of Mexico.

It has a unique hunting technique—the turtle lies motionless at the bottom of a river, mouth wide open, waving a bright red, worm-shaped projection located in the back of its mouth that serves as a lure to a curious fish or frog.

The Alligator snapping turtle can stay underwater for forty to fifty minutes before coming up for air, and the male almost never comes on land, although the female will venture in a hundred feet or so to lay her eggs. It spends so much time in the water that algae can grow on the back of its shell.

< 151 >

Bee balm

A fragrant member of the mint family, Bee balm was traditionally used as seasoning and an aid for digestive problems; Oswego tea, made from the leaves of the plant, was used by settlers who did not have access to English teas following the Boston Tea Party.

< The Lower Midwest: Catalpa >

Bee balm is the natural source of the antiseptic thymol, the main active ingredient in modern mouthwashes. Several American Indian tribes made use of the plant's strong antiseptic qualities, treating mouth and throat infections, minor wounds, skin infections, headaches and fever.

American badger

The American badger is described as *fossorial*, which means it spends most of its time underground. It is found most often in non-forested areas where, with its strong front legs and long sharp claws, it is very effective at digging dens and burrows. In summer, it may dig a new burrow each day.

The badger is such a quick, efficient excavator that it can easily dig a rodent out of its burrow. An apparently cooperative hunting effort with the coyote has evolved, in which the coyote chases the rodent underground, whereupon the badger attacks the burrow. In its attempt to escape the badger, the rodent runs back out. What the badger doesn't get, the coyote does. Badgers and coyotes tolerate each other's presence and have occasionally been observed playing together.

< 152 >

Texas blue bonnet

A native Texan will be proud to tell you that theirs was the first state to plant flowers alongside highways, and there are even a number of specially designated "Bluebonnet Trails" where this brightly colored flower is especially abundant.

The Texas bluebonnet is a species of lupin, a family with nearly 300 members. Though some lupins contain toxic alkaloids, several species are becoming increasingly valued as an alternative crop to soybeans. Cultivation of lupines is thought to have begun in the Mediterranean region, at least 2000 years ago.

Lupin seeds contain the full range of essential amino acids, and can be grown in a greater variety of climates and soils. The plant can also fix nitrogen, making it a good fertilizer, as well as a plant that helps make poor quality soils more fertile.

American Robin

The largest of the North American thrushes, the American Robin is a social bird. In

< Secret Voices from the Forest - Volume II >

summer, females sleep at their nests, while the males gather together in a large group (called a *mutation*) at roosts in nearby secluded trees. When all the young robins have left the nest, the females join the males at the roost. These large groups of robins can be huge, in winter numbering a quarter-million birds.

Hoary puccoon

The word "puccoon" is an Algonquin word for a number of different plants that were made into dye, which was used for pottery, basketry and personal ornamentation.

Barn Owl

Barn Owls have excellent low-light vision, and can easily find prey at night by sight. But their ability to locate prey by sound alone is the best of any animal that has ever been tested. They can catch mice in complete darkness, even hidden by vegetation or snow.

They nest in tree cavities, caves, and in any kind of human structure, including barn lofts, church steeples, houses, nest boxes, haystacks, and even drive-in movie screens and major league baseball stadiums.

Red Lovegrass

Worldwide, there are a great number of species of *Eragrostis*, or lovegrass, many of which have value for wildlife as food or cover. Their seeds are not usually used by humans for food, due to their extremely small size. However, certain species have been planted to prevent soil erosion, and in some cases as *hyperaccumulators*, to aid in environmental reclamation, because their roots can absorb heavy metals and toxic radioactive particles from the soil without harm to the plant, storing them in their stems and leaves.

< 153 >

< The Lower Midwest: Catalpa >

⦊ PERSIMMON ⦉

REFLECTIONS on THE INESTIMABLE VALUE

What Persimmon Can Tell You About Itself

I am witness to the greatness of the Galaxy, which becomes visible only during the hours of darkness, and the way in which it is reflected in our own sphere. When you know, as I do, that size does not matter, you realize that all things, in relation to each other, are of equal measure. I perceive the *true* worth, the *Inestimable Value* of each part of creation, in both the large and the small.

Nothing craves appreciation more than the stars. This is not vanity on their part, as their effect on us is more profound than you may think—they are our ancestors, and perhaps our future. By marking their passage in my skin (you have to know where to look), I am making a record of them. I often dream about following them, on their path through the heavens, to some remote galaxy. Since I am afraid of becoming lost, I don't go, so I admire that you try.

On the other end of the scale, the ants understand the importance of creating and maintaining order and structure, although they require no acknowledgement from you or me.

Wild cattle, and other herd animals, can give us insight into the ways of the group mind, and how we may all be affected by it, without knowing. On the other side of that coin, there is an appreciation of companions, who give us comfort, security, and a sense of deep belonging. This is an important thing to know in a time when futility and lack of possibility hang over us like a dark cloud.

We trees try to balance any unpleasant sensation by creating steadiness around us, by neutralizing impurities in the air, earth and water. Here in the Lower Midwest, the land gives us its patronage, supporting and facilitating our continued growth.

Persimmon's Place in the World

We are members of the Ebony Family, so we appreciate darkness, and know what it is that makes the sky black—the sky loves light so much that it absorbs it. When the resulting "love child" bursts forth, it has become bright colorful gases and stars, which explode out into the universe as love. Persimmons are stargazers, not star-voyagers, but we have a particular regard for those shining lights and colors.

Persimmon has come to know that this planet is well loved by the parent galaxy, and will be protected from destruction, although not from superficial damage. We, as a species, hope to pass on a curiosity about life, and a desire to investigate, for discovery and discernment are the first steps in understanding Inestimable Value.

Persimmon's Message to Us

Learn to be calm and accepting of events that seem arbitrary, as you have often been instrumental setting them in motion, and resistance will only make the circumstances that have arisen that much more difficult to endure.

You have a gift for organization, and for dividing things into groups and giving them names. As tools to accompany this, you have invented devices and methods to mark time, and of recording events as they occur, in clocks, calendars, words and language. Remember, though, that these things are ultimately impermanent, so don't devote excessive amounts of your own precious time to things of inconsequence. Part of the incessant triviality of your lives is due to an in-turning, cannibalistic usage of your group energy.

You have a great capacity for generosity of spirit. In times of disaster or great need, the artificial, separating barriers you have erected within and around your species come down, and you extend your compassion and abilities to other life forms on the Earth. This is happening more and more, though this awakening to humility is still in its adolescence. Humility is not so much a feeling of insignificance, or lesser value, as it is being aware of the worth of others, and that the loss of any one thing will be felt.

CHRONICLES

< 157 >

The sweet, orange fruit of this tree is only edible when it has become so ripe that it falls from the tree, at which point it is considered to be, as its genus name, *Diospyros*, asserts, "fruit of the gods."

The American persimmon is a member of the Ebony family, as are its close relations: the Black sapote, found in Mexico, Central and South America, the Kaki, from Japan, and

< The Lower Midwest: Persimmon >

the Ebony itself, from India. Fruit from cultivars of the Kaki are the kind found in your market. They became popular in the late 19th century, after Western trade relations with Japan were renewed. They are much larger than North American persimmons, which only reach the size of an apricot.

Seeds of the American persimmon were brought to England before or during the 17th century, and while the tree grows well there, its fruits rarely ripen.

While the American species does not have a commercial following, its fruit is still eaten extensively by a long list of wildlife, including a dozen species of birds, opossums—who like them so much the tree is called "Possumwood" in some areas—black bears, who will climb the trees to reach the sweet fruit, and White-tailed deer, who are not only excessively fond of the fruits, ripe or not, but browse on leaves and twigs during fall and winter, as well as by the people who are fortunate enough to have these lovely trees on their property.

< 158 >

Although deer can consume parts of the persimmon other than ripe fruit, domesticated animals are unable to eat it without becoming ill. Leaves, twigs, and unripe fruit contain a soluble tannin which, when combined with stomach acid, can produce a gluey substance that affixes to other stomach contents, forming a small stone-like object called a *bezoar*, an item known to many of us from the *Harry Potter* books. Bezoar is a Persian word that means "antidote." At one time, bezoars were prized as a ubiquitous remedy for poison. In 1575, surgeon Ambroise Paré tested this assertion by giving one to a criminal who was awaiting execution by hanging. The man died in excruciating pain several hours later, disproving the claim for good.

Some scientists believe that persimmon was one of the favored foods of the large animals that roamed the North American grasslands before the last glacial period ended, such as the Mastodon, Giant sloth, Saiga antelope, and others. For trees with an extensive range during the late Pleistocene, the disappearance of these *megafauna*, which had spread their seeds,

< Secret Voices from the Forest - Volume II >

spelled a reduction in range, as today's plant eating species find them inedible. Although one of the trees in this category, the persimmon's distribution has fared better, even spreading since that era. This is partially due to the large variety of birds and animals that eat their fruits, as well as to deliberate planting by Indians, to whom persimmons were a reliable source of food.

The first Europeans were introduced to Indian persimmon "bread," which was a sun-dried loaf of persimmon mash. This early food was modernized by the addition of various flours and spices. There are many recipes for custards and puddings, candy, beer, wine, and brandy, which is known as "possum toddy" by U.S. Southerners.

As the American Civil War dragged on, citizens of the Confederacy had difficulty obtaining common items because of blockades. The lack of coffee was felt particularly keenly. It seems that many (like myself) agreed with the opinion that coffee is "one of the chief necessities of life." Early instructions on coffee roasting warned against excessive heat, as burnt beans made a beverage similar to "an infusion of charred wood."

Many products were ground and roasted to use as coffee substitutes, such as chicory root, dandelion seed, sweet potatoes, peanuts, rice, and persimmon seeds which, apparently, were sufficient unto the task. On November 18, 1863, Alabama's *Montgomery Weekly Advertiser* wrote, "The seeds of the persimmon, when roasted and ground, produce a beverage, which cannot, even by old and experienced coffee drinkers, be distinguished from genuine coffee. We wish some of our lady readers would try the experiment and inform us as to the result." The same paper reported that a family in Brooklyn suffered toxic effects from drinking rye coffee, another traditional substitute. The Health Officer doing the investigation concluded they had been victims of ergot poisoning.

Persimmon wood is smooth, dense and almost black. It has been used to make products that need to be hard and strong, such as golf clubs called "woods," shoe lasts, which traditionally are wooden models of the human foot, used to make shoes, as well as mallets, screws, textile shuttles, and more recently, by bow craftsmen, to make classic longbows.

PERSIMMON COMPANIONS

Eastern Green Toad
Pine Woods Lily
Flammulina Velutipes
Luna Moth
Spotted Touch-me-not
Bald Eagle
June Grass
Ozark Hellbender
Jack-in-the-pulpit
Coyote Thistle
Eastern Pipistrelle Bat
Osage Copperhead
White Milkweed
Painted Bunting
Corkwood
Raccoon
3-Birds Orchid
American Burying Beetle

Food of the Gods, it is said,
and why not, if gods still sail
purposefully across galaxies?
For when the setting sun
floods the lone horizon with colors
deepening into dark, and stars
crowd into Heaven's hall,
each bearing endurances of time
too vast for knowing, their grave
regarding light lands like manna
on my sleeping leaves
and it is ecstasy. Ecstasy.
Now let drop the fullripe fruit!

First stage falling away.

FACTS ABOUT SOME PERSIMMON COMPANIONS

Bald Eagle

The Bald Eagle is a "sea eagle," making its nest near lakes and rivers. Unique to North America, it is has been a spiritual symbol to many of the continent's First People for hundreds of years, and became the national emblem for the United States in 1782.

"Bald" once was the term for "white." An immature Bald Eagle does not develop white feathers on its head until after the age of four, and may spend the first four years of their lives wandering, covering distances of over 1,300 miles.

At about ten pounds, the Bald Eagle is a heavy bird, second only to the California Condor in size, but its skeleton only weighs about a half pound; its feathers weigh twice that much. A Bald Eagle has some 7,000 strong, lightweight feathers to protect it from cold. It will move to find better food resources, but not to avoid cold weather.

Eagle wing feathers are long and broad, with tapered tips that separate and reduce turbulence, which helps the eagle soar. Using rising currents of warm air, and updrafts created by variances in terrain, an eagle is able to soar long distances with very little effort. It can reach an altitude of 10,000 feet, and several eagles soaring in a thermal column of air together is termed a "kettle of eagles." The Bald Eagle has a spectacular courting ritual. The couple flies high into the sky, where they lock talons and plummet to the ground, breaking off at the last instant to avoid crashing.

A lone eagle feather is believed to convey great power, and Indians incorporated the eagle's wing and tail feathers into their ceremonies and legends.

Velvet-foot fungus

Velvet-foot fungus is one of the few edible mushrooms that can be found in the winter, outside of the West and Gulf Coasts.

A form of this mushroom cultivated by the Japanese is called *Enoki* or *Enokitake*, and can be found in specialty grocery stores and restaurants. As it is grown in jars in the dark, forcing it to grow long and thin, it bears no resemblance to the wild form.

In 1994 *Flammulina velutipes* was cultivated on the Space Shuttle Columbia, in order to see the effects of weightlessness on the directional growth of its stems. Lack of gravity disoriented the mushroom, and its stems, instead of growing straight up, grew in all directions at once.

< Secret Voices from the Forest - Volume II >

< 162 >

American burying beetle

The American burying beetle flies at night, locating the carcasses of birds and small mammals within an hour of death, and from as far away as two miles, with olfactory organs located in their antennae. It is important that they find the animal quickly, before flies arrive to lay their eggs.

After they find the body, it is buried by digging out the soil from underneath. If the soil at the location is too hard, the beetles may move the carcass several feet by lying on their backs with it balanced above them, walking their legs to move it forward to softer ground. After the body is below the surface, the beetles remove fur and feathers and secrete a substance that retards decomposition. Several inches of soil are placed on top, with a small chamber on top where the female lays up to thirty eggs.

When the larvae have hatched, both parents care for them and assist them in their feeding for six to twelve days, behavior normally found only in social insects. After the larvae have consumed everything but the bones, the adults fly away and die soon after. The young pupate in the nearby soil, emerging a month later. They will overwinter as adults, buried in the ground.

< 163 >

Spotted jewelweed

Also called Touch-me-not, this flower contains a juice reported to relieve the sting from Poison ivy, stinging nettle, bug bites and burns, similar to the effects of aloe vera. It also has fungicidal qualities and has been used to treat athlete's foot.

The Spotted jewelweed is called touch-me-not because its elongated seedpod opens explosively at the slightest touch, sending seeds up to four feet away.

Luna moth

Luna moths are members of the *Saturniidae* family, a.k.a. "Giant Silkworm moths." Large, with a wingspan of four and a half inches, they fly only at night, in spring and early summer, to find mates. Adult Luna moths have no mouths and do not eat; they live only for a week—long enough to mate and lay eggs.

The caterpillars eat the leaves of a variety of trees, including white birch, sweet gum, walnuts, hickories and pecans, sumacs and persimmons.

< The Lower Midwest: Persimmon >

In the symbolism of animals, butterflies are of the day and the sun; moths are of the night and the moon. Therefore, do not necessarily believe what is presented to you; look for hidden meanings. Look to your dreams or intuitive impulses for answers and guidance.

Jack-in-the-pulpit

Like the Skunk cabbage, philodendron, Dieffenbachia, peace-lily and Calla lily, the Jack-in-the-pulpit is a member of the Arum family, and it has an uncommon structure. The funnel-like part we see is a modified leaf called the *spathe*, which confines pollinating fungus gnats and small flies, and protects the *spadix*, an erect cylinder from which tiny flowers emerge. A swollen section of the stem, called a *corm*, is underground, and acts as a food reservoir.

A seedling spends from four to six years in an immature state, finally producing male flowers that produce pollen. As the plant ages — the corm can live for 100 years — the spadix, which increases in size over time, begins to produce female flowers, which can produce seeds and fruit. However, if there are environmental stresses or if food stores in the corm are insufficient, the female plant will revert back to its male form, or even back to the pre-flowering, vegetative state. This process is called *sequential hermaphroditism*. It ensures the genetic quality of the plant and uses energy efficiently during times of scarcity.

In spite of containing a toxic level of oxalic acid, American Indians had many uses for this plant, including producing red dye and a topical painkiller. Powdered corm dissolved in water was used as a means of contraception — one dose worked for a week and two doses produced permanent sterility.

Raccoon

Raccoons will eat just about anything, from insects, land and aquatic animals, to fruit and even trash. They are found almost everywhere — forests, marshes, prairies, as well as cities. In some states, they are more populous in cities than in the wild.

Their human-like forepaws make them good at grabbing, holding, pulling apart and opening. They are also adept climbers, and are one of the few animals able to come down a tree headfirst.

Raccoons have exceptional night vision and a heightened sense of hearing, so they mate, hunt, and forage mostly at night.

3-Birds orchid

This rare orchid favors old beech and maple forests, growing underground, sometimes for years without flowering, in close association with certain types of fungi. Then, in late July or early August, after the rains have come and the nights begin to cool, when conditions are right, the plant sends up a tiny green stalk with three buds.

The blooming time is short, sometimes only lasting a few days, often forming a "fairy ring" around an old beech or Sugar maple. All the plants bloom at once, wilt and go to seed; then in a few days will bud and bloom again, until by early September they are gone, impossible to find until they choose to bloom again.

Ozark Hellbender

The Ozark hellbender is a large, nocturnal, aquatic salamander found only in southern Missouri and northern Arkansas, growing up to two feet long. Its flattened body shape enables it to move in fast flowing streams. It is long-lived, becoming sexually mature at five to eight years of age and surviving up to thirty years in the wild.

Because hellbenders breathe entirely through their skin, they need cool, clear streams and rivers with many sizable rocks. Both larvae and adults spend most of their life under large, flat rocks that shelter them.

Recently, a highly infectious disease, the chytrid fungus, has been found in the Missouri populations. It is proving fatal to an ever-increasing number of amphibians throughout the world and has been found in all remaining Ozark hellbender populations in Missouri. It is thought that this disease may be responsible for the worldwide amphibian decline.

With fewer than six hundred of these amphibians remaining in existence, in October, 2011, the U.S. Fish and Wildlife Service listed the Ozark hellbender as an endangered species. The Saint Louis Zoo and the Missouri Department of Conservation have spent fifteen years collaborating on breeding the species in captivity, with great success. Rivers in south-central Missouri and adjacent Arkansas once supported up to eight thousand Ozark hellbenders. Once these captive-bred larvae are three to eight years old, they can then be released into their natural habitat—the Ozark aquatic ecosystem.

NON-CONFRONTATIONAL ACTIVISM

As governments have learned over the millennia, when an element of society is depersonalized, it becomes acceptable to utilize, abuse, or even exterminate that element, because it has no relationship to *you*. It's the same with plants. Nothing is really a "weed"—it's just a plant we want to remove so we can put in something else that we think will be of more benefit to *us*. Historically, we have related to trees as a "product" or a "cash crop," or, only a little less self-interested, something beautiful that should be preserved for the enjoyment of *our* future generations.

Many of us don't have the emotional constitution to be activists, assaulting, or being assaulted with blame and recrimination, aimed at shaming us into behaving differently. The reaction to shame is variable. At best, it inspires the usually short-lived zeal of the newly converted, or perhaps reluctant accommodation; at worst, it urges one to deliberate opposition. Even those that are sympathetic, but not on the front lines, are relentlessly bombarded with bad news, and then even *worse* news. We're exhausted. We need a break! Don't these guys realize that 99% of the time they're preaching to the choir?

The Green movement has just started to go mainstream. Many more of us desire to learn ways to make a lesser impact on the earth. So can't it be easier?

I'm not sticking my head in the sand. I just don't think the way to get more people to change their ways is to continuously attempt to shame them. I think the old saying of "you catch more flies with honey than vinegar" applies here. If people enjoy being in nature, if they can relate to trees, for instance, as they would another person, maybe as a friend, then perhaps they'll be more willing to make some lifestyle sacrifices for the sake of trees.

< 167 >

Or, put another way, the wise have long understood that in order to gain sympathy, you must first engender empathy. So, why *not* personalize Nature? I'm not advocating that we picture plants and animals with human features and abilities, or imagine that they have the same attitudes and problems as we. Rather, we might consider them as something entirely *other*, with totally different methods of perceiving and relating to existence.

I'm not trying to say we shouldn't eat, or build our houses out of wood, or find energy sources to power our lives and our cities. Joseph Campbell talked about the dilemma that faced primitive cultures: they had to kill in order to stay alive. In order to cope with their uncomfortable feelings, a family provider would thank the animal or the plant for assisting him in feeding his family. The animal or plant *itself* was a representative of The Divine, regarded as a God incarnate, blessing the tribe with the gift of Life.

Civilization may be a bit far along to go back entirely to that approach, but the fact that many people talk to their plants to make them grow, and treat their pets better than they do their children, points to the possibility that it's really quite a short step for the rest of us to think of trees as sentient, as our neighbors, or even as our friends.

< The Lower Midwest >

SOURCES CITED

The websites listed here are intended for use by anyone who may be interested in further information on a referenced subject. There is no guarantee that these websites, as listed, will still be functional at the time of reading. In some cases, the website will have been updated and the web address changed, in which case a site may be relocated through a subject search.

CHAPTER ONE—GREAT PLAINS

The Geologic Story of The Great Plains, A nontechnical description of the origin and evolution of the landscape of the Great Plains Trimble, Donald E., Geological Survey Bulletin 1493, United States Government Printing Office, Washington, D.C.: 1980, Scanned and formatted by Kathryn Thomas, North Dakota State University Libraries - February 9, 1999, http://www.lib.ndsu.nodak.edu/govdocs/text/greatplains/text.html; *Prairie, A Natural History*, Savage, Candace. 2004, Vancouver, British Columbia, CA: Greystone Books, Douglas and McIntyre, Ltd.

< 168 >

American Elm

"Ulmus americana is a polyploid complex", Whittemore, Alan T., and Richard T. Olsen, 2011. *Journal of Botanical Research Institute of Texas*, 98(4): 754-760; "The Curious Case of the Washington Elms That Are Unlike Any Other", By KENNETH CHANG. Published: April 4, 2011, New York Times; "Scientists breed supertrees to beat Dutch elm", BY THE OTTAWA CITIZEN SEPTEMBER 11, 2007© (c) CanWest MediaWorks Publications Inc.; • http://www.ars.usda.gov/is/pr/2011/110330.htm; • http://www.gardenguides.com/129046-life-cycle-american-elm-tree.html#ixzz2N52YQdbV; • http://classwebs.spea.indiana.edu/bakerr/v600/rachel_carson_and_silent_spring.htm; • http://theborderlife.com/Elm-Tree.php; • *Silent Spring*, Carson, Rachel. Boston, MA: HOUGHTON MIFFLIN HARCOURT; Book Club edition (1962); • *The Republic of Shade: New England and the American Elm*, Thomas J. Campanella, 2003, New Haven CT: Yale University Press.

Elm companions

http://www.defenders.org/bison/basic-facts; • http://www.wcs.org/saving-wildlife/hoofed-mammals/bison/the-american-bison-society.aspx; • http://www.yvwiiusdinvnohii.net/lit/bufwoman.htm; • http://www.aihd.ku.edu/foods/arrowhead.html; • http://www.billcasselman.com/casselmans_canadian_words/ccw_six.htm;http://www.wiseacre-gardens.com/plants/wildflower/arrowhead.html; • http://buzz.ifas.ufl.edu/; • http://www.entnemdept.ufl.edu/walker/buzz/ •

http://www.musicofnature.org/songsofinsects/iframes/specieslist.html; • http://www.gpnc.org/field1.htm; • http://www.arkive.org/field-cricket/gryllus-campestris/; • Varro Tyler, PhD. *Tyler's Herbs of Choice: The Therapeutic Use of Phytomedicinals*. Oxford, United Kingdom, Routledge 1999. http://botanical.com/botanical/mgmh/i/ivypoi17.html; • http://botanical.com/botanical/mgmh/i/ivypoi17.html; • http://operationmigration.org; • http://flower—pot.blogspot.com/2012/01/synstylae-species.html;http://www.antiqueroseemporium.com/roses/119/prairie-rose;http://davesgarden.

< Secret Voices from the Forest - Volume II >

com/guides/articles/view/710/#b; • Walker, Barbara G. *The Woman's Encyclopedia of Myths and Secrets*. San Francisco, CA: HarperSanFrancisco, 1983. p. 866-69; • http://www.gpnc.org/mouseng. htm; • http://fieldguide.mt.gov/detail_AMAFF06010.aspx; • http://www.webmd.com/food-recipes/ news/20090203/mushrooms-cut-grapefruit-drug-effect •

Boxelder

https://www.uwgb.edu/biodiversity/herbarium/trees/aceneg01.htm; • http://www. missouribotanicalgarden.org/gardens-gardening/your-garden/plant-finder/plant-details/kc/a841/ acer-negundo.aspx; • http://www.museum.state.il.us/muslink/forest/htmls/trees/A-negundo.html; • http://www.fs.fed.us/database/feis/plants/tree/aceneg/all.html; • http://www.aluaki.com/the-term—anasazi.php; • http://www.native-languages.org/flutes.htm; • http://hewit.unco.edu/DOHIST/ puebloan/context/archmenu.htm; • http://www.cpluhna.nau.edu/People/anasazi.htm; • http:// www.kidport.com/RefLib/SocialStudies/NativeAmericans/Pueblo.htm; • http://www.solsticeproject. org/primarch.htm; • http://www.britannica.com/EBchecked/topic/22804/Ancestral-Pueblo-culture; • http://www.nps.gov/chcu/historyculture/chacoan-roads.htm •

Boxelder companions

http://www.na.fs.fed.us/pubs/silvics_manual/volume_2/quercus/macrocarpa.htm; • http://articles. chicagotribune.com/2012-04-19/classified/ct-sun-garden-0422-morton-bur-oak-20120419_1_bur-oak-tallgrass-prairies-tough-tree; • http://www.squidoo.com/oaktrees; • http://www.azgfd.gov/w_c/ blackfooted_ferret.shtml; • http://nationalzoo.si.edu/SCBI/reproductivescience/recoverbfferret/ default.cfm; • http://www1.extension.umn.edu/garden/insects/find/boxelder-bugs/; • http:// www.nbcchicago.com/news/local/Drought-to-Blame-for-Boxelder-Bug-Influx-174795061. html#ixzz2D48XhQaP; • http://botit.botany.wisc.edu/toms_fungi/may2001.html; • http://www. gpnc.org/ornate.htm; • http://www.fs.fed.us/r2/projects/scp/assessments/ornateboxturtle.pdf; • Read more: http://www.motherearthnews.com/Organic-Gardening/1982-09-01/Wild-Gooseberries-and-Currants.aspx?page=4#ixzz2D4jB3W4u; • http://www.fws.gov/mountain-prairie/species/ mammals/btprairiedog/; • http://www.defenders.org/prairie-dogs/prairie-dogs-101; • http://www. nhptv.org/natureworks/blacktailedpraire.htm; • http://www.wildflower.org/plants/result.php?id_ plant=HEAN3; • http://www.gpnc.org/sunflower.htm; • http://birds.audubon.org/birds/red-eyed-vireo •

American Plum

http://www.dnr.state.oh.us/Home/trees/plum_american/tabid/5413/Default.aspx; • http://www. kansasforests.org/conservation/shrubs/americanplum.shtml; • http://medplant.nmsu.edu/wildplum. shtml; • http://www.lib.ksu.edu/wildflower/wildplum.html; • http://www.exnet.iastate.edu/Pages/ tree/plum.html; • Gilmore, Melvin R. 1919 Uses of Plants by the Indians of the Missouri River Region. SI-BAE Annual Report #33 (p. 87); • Tantaquidgeon, Gladys 1972 Folk Medicine of the Delaware and Related Algonkian Indians. Harrisburg. Pennsylvania Historical Commission Anthropological Papers #3 (p. 87); • http://www.sacred-texts.com/nam/pla/sdo/sdo03.htm - original source: Anthropological Papers of the American Museum of Natural History, Volume XVI, Part II: The Sun Dance and Other Ceremonies of the Oglala Division of the Teton Dakota," by J.R. Walker. New York: The American Museum of Natural History, Published by order of the trustees, 1917. Scanned at Sacred-texts.com, November 2002. J.B. Hare, Redactor •

Plum companions

http://www.native-languages.org/legends-grasshopper.htm; • http://www.umm.edu/altmed/ articles/dandelion-000236.htm#ixzz2CbehbQnK; • http://www.umm.edu/altmed/articles/ dandelion-000236.htm; • http://botanical.com/botanical/mgmh/d/dandel08.html; • http://www.

defenders.org/swift-fox/basic-facts; • http://raysweb.net/specialplaces/pages/fox.html; • http://www.blueplanetbiomes.org/swift_fox.htm; • http://www.endangeredwolfcenter.org/learn/canid-encyclopedia/swift-fox; • http://www.americanprairie.org/projectprogress/science-and-wildlife/swift-fox-reintroduction-and-study/; • http://www.blueplanetbiomes.org/pasque_flower.htm; • http://www.illinoiswildflowers.info/prairie/plantx/pasqueflower.htm;http://www.netstate.com/states/symb/flowers/sd_pasque_flower.ht;http://truedakotan.com/news/sd-magazine-how-south-dakotan-are-you/; • http://www.allaboutbirds.org/guide/Wild_Turkey/id; • http://www.nwtf.org/all_about_turkeys/wild_turkey_facts.html; • http://www.basspro.com/webapp/wcs/stores/servlet/CFPageCstoreId=10151&catalogId=10001&langId=-1&&mode=article&objectID=32138&catID=&subcatID=0; • http://www.fcps.edu/islandcreekes/ecology/wild_turkey.htm; • http://www.texasbeyondhistory.net/tejas/voices/today.html; • Public television aired a lovely episode of *Nature*, called, "My Life as a Turkey," in November of 2012--worth seeing: http://www.pbs.org/wnet/nature/category/episodes/by-animal/turkey/; • http://inventors.about.com/library/weekly/aa091297.htm; • http://animaldiversity.ummz.umich.edu/accounts/Sander_vitreus/; • http://www.easywildflowers.com/quality/Rat.col.htm; • http://www.gardensablaze.com/WildflowersMexHat.htm; • http://www.gardeningclub.com/gardening/articletype/articleview/articleid/378/mexican-hat; • http://www.kansasnativeplantsociety.org/wfoy_2011.php; • http://www.wisegeek.com/what-is-a-mexican-hat-plant.htm#lbss; • http://www.iucnredlist.org/details/14132/0; • http://www.fws.gov/midwest/endangered/mammals/grbat_fc.html; • http://www.kdwpt.state.ks.us/news/Services/Threatened-and-Endangered-Wildlife/Threatened-and-Endangered-Species/Species-Information/GRAY-MYOTIS; • http://www.pitt.edu/~cjm6/w98echin.html, Bonnie K. McMillen, Bonnie K., and Carol J. Mulvihill, University of Pittsburgh at Bradford ; • http://www.legendsofamerica.com/na-herbs4.html#E ; • http://www.gardensalive.com/article.asp?ai=804 •

CHAPTER TWO — GREAT LAKES

http://www.epa.gov/greatlakes/basicinfo.html; • http://www.great-lakes.net; • http://www.newgeology.us/presentation41.html; • http://www.canadianshieldfoundation.ca/?page_id=39; • http://polarmet.osu.edu/PolarMet/paleonwp.html; • http://www.worldislandinfo.com/GreatLakes.htm •

American Basswood

http://www.courierpress.com/news/2008/may/25/family-still-tends-ww-i-peace-tree/; • http://www.drgrotte.com/honey-medicine.shtml; • http://plants.usda.gov/plantguide/pdf/cs_tiama.pdf; • http://forestry.about.com/od/hardwoods/tp/American_Basswood.htm; • http://ohiodnr.com/forestry/trees/bass_amr/tabid/5335/Default.aspx; • http://www.honeytraveler.com/single-flower-honey/linden-lime-basswood-honey/; • http://www.med-honey.com/english/lipov_med.php; • http://keepingbee.org/linden-honey/; • n more: http://www.naturalnews.com/021506_honey_grocery_healing.html#ixzz2Su1Wr6Cx; • http://www.crandallfarms.com/benefits.html; • http://www.bee-hexagon.net/files/file/fileE/HealthHoney/9HoneyMedicineReview.pdf •

Basswood companions

http://www.allaboutbirds.org/guide/Belted_Kingfisher/lifehistory; • http://birds.audubon.org/species/belkin; • www.beakspeak.com; • http://www.fcps.edu/islandcreekes/ecology/belted_kingfisher.htm; • http://www.bio.umass.edu/biology/conn.river/beltedkingfishe.html; • http://www.thefineprintuf.org/2012/03/17/city-farmer-the-willow-trees-secrets/; • http://inventors.about.com/library/inventors/blaspirin.htm; • http://www.fcps.edu/islandcreekes/ecology/bullfrog.htm; • http://allaboutfrogs.org/info/species/bullfrog.html; • http://naturemappingfoundation.org/natmap/facts/american_bullfrog_712.html; • http://www.fs.fed.us/wildflowers/plant-of-the-week/cypripedium_acaule.shtml; • http://www.fcps.edu/islandcreekes/ecology/pink_ladys_slipper.htm; • http://www.50states.com/flower/minnesota.htm; • http://www.timberwolfinformation.org/

kidsonly/wolfweb/wolf.htm; • http://www.wolf.org/wolves/learn/basic/wolf_types/inter_gray/
timber.asp; • http://www.buzzle.com/articles/eastern-timber-wolf.html; • http://www.timberwolfps.
org/wolf-facts.html; • http://www.wolfcountry.net/information/WolfObserved.html; • http://www.
blueplanetbiomes.org/big_bluestem_grass.htm; • http://www.outsidepride.com/seed/native-grass-
seed/bluestem-big-native-grass-seed.html; • http://www.illinoiswildflowers.info/grasses/plants/
bigblue.htm; • http://www.silkmoths.bizland.com/hthysbe.htm; • http://www.fs.fed.us/wildflowers/
pollinators/pollinator-of-the-month/hummingbird_moth.shtml; • http://www.enature.com/
fieldguides/detail.asp?recNum=TS0276; • http://animalrangeextension.montana.edu/articles/forage/
Plants/Chokecherry.htm; • http://www.cirrusimage.com/Hymenoptera_bumble_bee_tricolored.htm; •
http://www.xerces.org/spring-ahead-with-bumble-bee-garden-kits/; • http://botit.botany.wisc.edu/
toms_fungi/apr2006.html; • http://www.mushroomexpert.com/aleurodiscus_oakesii.html •

White Spruce/Black Spruce

http://www.conifers.org/pi/Picea_glauca.phpPicea glauca (Moench) Voss; • http://www.wildflower.
org/plants/result.php?id_plant=PIGL; • http://www.dnr.state.mn.us/trees_shrubs/conifers/
blackspruce.html; • http://www.uwgb.edu/biodiversity/herbarium/gymnosperms/picmar01.htm;
• http://northernwoodlands.org/knots_and_bolts/spruce-up-your-id-skills; • http://www.pfaf.org/
user/Plant.aspx?LatinName=Picea+mariana •

Spruce companions

http://animals.nationalgeographic.com/animals/amphibians/mudpuppy/ http://www.michigan.gov/
dnr/0,4570,7-153-10364_18958-35084—,00.html; • http://home.howstuffworks.com/define-helenium-
sneezeweed.htm; • http://www.wildflower.org/plants/result.php?id_plant=HEAU; • http://www.
portlandnursery.com/plants/perennials/helenium.shtml; • http://www.allaboutbirds.org/guide/
Common_Loon/lifehistory; • http://animals.nationalgeographic.com/animals/birds/common-loon/;
• http://www.dnr.state.mn.us/birds/commonloon.html; • http://www.wcs.org/saving-wildlife/
birds/common-loon.aspx; • http://www.fcps.edu/islandcreekes/ecology/highbush_blueberry.htm;
• http://www.wildflower.org/plants/result.php?id_plant=VACO; • http://www.blueberrycouncil.
org/blueberry-facts/history-of-blueberries/; • http://scienceblogs.com/neurophilosophy/2009/08/26/
the-star-nosed-moles-amazing-appendages/; • http://www.pbs.org/wnet/nature/episodes/the-
beauty-of-ugly/star-nosed-moles/428/; • http://www.esf.edu/aec/adks/mammals/starnosed_mole.
htmhttp://www.naturalhistorymag.com/picks-from-the-past/201397/a-star-is-born?page=4; •
http://www.nativeorchid.org/news200604.htm#OOM; • http://www.wildflower.org/plants/result.
php?id_plant=COMA25; • http://www.swcoloradowildflowers.com/White%20Enlarged%20Photo%20
Pages/corallorhiza.htm; • http://ohiodnr.com/Portals/3/Abstracts/Abstract_pdf/C/Corallorhiza_
maculata.pdf; • http://www.britannica.com/EBchecked/topic/636982/water-boatman; • http://
www.everythingabout.net/articles/biology/animals/arthropods/insects/bugs/water_boatman/; •
http://www.bbc.co.uk/nature/; • http://www.plosone.org/article/info:doi%2F10.1371%2Fjournal.
pone.002108913958630; • http://www.outdoors.org/conservation/mountainwatch/painted-trillium.
cfm; • http://www.bluewateraudubon.50megs.com/painted%20trillium%20project.html; • http://
www.woodturtle.com/Description.html; • http://www.turtleconservationproject.org/wood-turtle-facts.
html; • http://www.greenhopeessences.com/Essences/Farm/blueflagiris.htm; • http://www.seagrant.
wisc.edu/greatlakesfish/musky.html; • http://www.michigan.gov/dnr/0,4570,7-153-10364_18958-
45684—,00.html; • http://www.merriam-webster.com/dictionary/muskellunge; • http://www.
michigan.gov/documents/dnr/Muskellunge_-_A_Michigan_Resource_-_May_2012_386501_7.pdf; •
http://www.efloras.org/florataxon.aspx?flora_id=1&taxon_id=105644; • http://systematics.mortonarb.
org/lab/publications/Hipp-et-al-2009_BotRev_CarexChromosomesReview.pdf •

Staghorn Sumac

http://www.wildflower.org/plants/result.php?id_plant=RHTY; • http://gardeningintunewithnature.

< 171 >

< Sources >

bangordailynews.com/2012/08/21/ornamentals/staghorn-sumac-a-tree-for-all-seasons/; •
http://winemaking.jackkeller.net/staghorn.asp; • http://herb.umd.umich.edu/herb/search.
pl?searchstring=Rhus+typhina; • http://foragingfamily.blogspot.com/2011/07/staghorn-sumac-rhus-
typhina-tart.html; • http://www.fs.fed.us/database/feis/plants/tree/rhutyp/all.html; • http://www.
missouribotanicalgarden.org/gardens-gardening/your-garden/plant-finder/plant-details/kc/c337/
rhus-typhina.aspx; • https://academics.skidmore.edu/wikis/NorthWoods/index.php/Rhus_typhina_
(Staghorn_Sumac); • http://www.huffingtonpost.com/2013/05/06/healthy-nuts-health-benefits-
cashews-walnuts-peanuts-almonds_n_3187731.html •

Sumac companions

http://www.allaboutbirds.org/guide/Barn_Swallow/lifehistory; • http://www.50birds.com/
BPBarnSwallow.htm; • http://www.ucan-online.org/legend.asp?legend=5706&category=3; •
http://hort.ufl.edu/database/documents/pdf/tree_fact_sheets/ptetria.pdf; • http://www.
wildflower.org/plants/result.php?id_plant=PTTR; • http://www.rom.on.ca/ontario/risk.php?doc_
type=fact&id=48&lang=en; • http://srelherp.uga.edu/salamanders/ambmac.htm; • http://www.
plantlife.org.uk/wild_plants/plant_species/grass-of-parnassus/; • http://www.mlahanas.de/Greeks/
Mythology/MountParnassus.html; • http://www.arkive.org/marsh-grass-of-parnassus/parnassia-
palustris/; • http://www.biokids.umich.edu/critters/Liochlorophis_vernalis/; • http://www3.
northern.edu/natsource/REPTILES/Greens1.htm; • http://www.lpzoo.org/animals/factsheet/
smooth-green-snake; • http://www.everything2.org/title/bulrush; • http://www.eattheweeds.com/
bulrush-bonanza/; • http://www.pittstate.edu/department/herbarium/common-grasses.dot; • http://
www.dnr.state.mn.us/mammals/canadalynx.html; • http://www.nwf.org/wildlife/wildlife-library/
mammals/canada-lynx.aspx; • http://www.maine.gov/ifw/wildlife/species/endangered_species/
canada_lynx/; • http://animals.nationalgeographic.com/animals/mammals/snowshoe-hare/; •
http://www.nwf.org/Wildlife/Wildlife-Library/Mammals/Snowshoe-Hare.aspx; • http://www.
hiltonpond.org/ThisWeek010608.html; • http://davesgarden.com/guides/pf/go/561/#b; • http://
www.wildflower.org/plants/result.php?id_plant=GAPR2; • http://keys2liberty.wordpress.com/tag/
spotted-wintergreen/; • http://botanical.com/botanical/mgmh/w/winter24.html; • http://animals.
nationalgeographic.com/animals/bugs/stick-insect/; • http://www.sandiegozoo.org/animalbytes/
t-stick_insect.html; • http://www.desertusa.com/animals/walking-stick.html;http://www.
findingdulcinea.com/features/science/environment/Parthenogenesis—When-Animals-Reproduce-
Without-a-Mate.html; • http://www.dickinsonbrands.com/about.htm ; • http://www.sierrapotomac.
org/W_Needham/Witch_Hazel_041003.htm ; • http://www.webmd.com/vitamins-supplements/
ingredientmono-227-WITCH%20HAZEL.aspx?activeIngredientId=227&activeIngredientName=WIT
CH%20HAZEL •

< 172 >

CHAPTER THREE—UPPER MIDWEST

http://fwp.mt.gov/mtoutdoors/HTML/articles/2005/MissouriSource.htm; • Lewis, Gene D. (1968).
Charles Ellet, Jr.: The Engineer as Individualist. University of Illinois Press; • http://www.nps.gov/
miss/riverfacts.htm; • © Dean Klinkenberg, 2011; • http://www.tulane.edu/~sanelson/Natural_
Disasters/riversystems.htm; • U.S. Geological Society; • Audubon Society •

Black Walnut

http://www.mrsoshouse.com/plants/walnut.html; • http://ohioline.osu.edu/hyg-fact/1000/1148.
html; • http://kniakrls.com/2013/05/des-moines-man-sentenced-for-theft-of-red-rock-walnut-trees/;
• www.sfp.forprod.vt.edu/factsheets/walnut.pdf; • http://www.webmd.com/vitamins-supplements/
ingredientmono-639-BLACK%20WALNUT.aspx?activeIngredientId=639&activeIngredientName=BL
ACK%20WALNUT; • http://faculty.ucc.edu/biology-ombrello/pow/black_walnut.htm; • http://
www.sciencemag.org/content/293/5532/1129.full; • Kurt O. Konhauser, et al. Aerobic bacterial pyrite

< Secret Voices from the Forest - Volume II >

oxidation and acid rock drainage during the Great Oxidation Event. Nature, 2011; • 478 (7369): 369 DOI: 10.1038/nature10511; • http://evolution.berkeley.edu/evolibrary/article/0_0_0/origsoflife_07 •

Walnut companions

http://www.allaboutbirds.org/guide/great_horned_owl/lifehistory; • http://animals.nationalgeographic.com/animals/birds/great-horned-owl/; • http://www.native-languages.org/legends-owl.htm; • http://www.ars.usda.gov/Services/docs.htm?docid=9943; • http://home.howstuffworks.com/delphinium-larkspur.htm; • http://www2.mcdaniel.edu/Biology/eco/mut/mutualism.html; • http://www.britannica.com/EBchecked/topic/399884/mutualism; • http://aggie-horticulture.tamu.edu/galveston/beneficials/beneficial-24_spider_blackandyellow_argiope.htm; • http://mdc.mo.gov/discover-nature/field-guide/black-and-yellow-garden-spider; • http://www.firstpeople.us; • http://www.abnativeplants.com/index.cfm?fuseaction=plants.plantdetail&plant_id=116; • http://forest.mtu.edu/kidscorner/ecosystems/dogwood.html; • http://www.academia.edu/279168/Botany_A_Record-Breaking_Pollen_Catapult; • http://fwp.mt.gov/mtoutdoors/HTML/articles/portraits/iowadarter.htm; • http://www.scientificamerican.com/article.cfm?id=grass-makes-better-ethanol-than-corn; • http://www.ernstseed.com/biomass/switchgrass-faqs/; • http://agroecology.clemson.edu/switchgrass/sg.htm; • http://www.allaboutbirds.org/guide/Blue_Jay/lifehistory; • http://animals.nationalgeographic.com/animals/birds/blue-jay/; • http://www.nhptv.org/natureworks/bluejay.htm; • http://www.fcps.edu/islandcreekes/ecology/blue_jay.htm; • http://www.fs.fed.us/wildflowers/plant-of-the-week/campanula_rotundifolia.shtml; • http://www.alchemy-works.com/campanula_rotundifolia.html; • Macdonald, David (1992). The Velvet Claw: A Natural History of the Carnivores. New York: Parkwest. ISBN 0-563-20844-9; Harris, Stephen; Yalden, Derek (2008). Mammals of the British Isles (4th Revised ed.). Mammal Society. ISBN 0-906282-65-9; http://www.worldoftales.com/Native_American_folktales/Native_American_Folktale_61.html •

Red Mulberry

< 173 >

https://edis.ifas.ufl.edu/fr326; • http://www.museum.state.il.us/muslink/forest/htmls/trees/M-rubra.html; • http://www.na.fs.fed.us/pubs/silvics_manual/volume_2/morus/rubra.htm; • http://www.wildmanstevebrill.com/Plants.Folder/Mulberries.html; • http://cdn.intechopen.com/pdfs/28744/InTech-Dietary_anthocyanins_impact_on_colorectal_cancer_and_mechanisms_of_action.pdf; • http://altmedicine.about.com/od/herbsupplementguide/a/The-Scoop-On-Anthocyanins.htm; • https://www.ncbi.nlm.nih.gov/pubmed/18288999; • http://pss.uvm.edu/ppp/pubs/oh24colr.htm; • http://www.gardeningknowhow.com/special/children/why-plants-have-bright-colored-flowers-flower-color-significance.htm; • http://www.ehow.com/about_6745567_do-plants-color_.html; • http://askingnlearning.com/blog/index.ph…; • https://www.ncbi.nlm.nih.gov/pubmed/18288999; • http://altmedicine.about.com/od/herbsupplementguide/a/The-Scoop-On-Anthocyanins.htm; • http://researchnews.osu.edu/archive/canberry.htm; • http://www.sciencedaily.com/releases/2010/04/100406125545.htm •

Mulberry companions

http://www.illinoiswildflowers.info/wetland/plants/pitcher_plant.htm; • http://wildflowers.jdcc.edu/Sarraceniaceae.html; • http://www.nature.com/news/earth-s-carbon-sink-downsized-1.11503; • http://littoralzone.wordpress.com/2008/06/12/acid-bogs-really-insanely-cool/#comment-154; • http://animals.nationalgeographic.com/animals/mammals/white-tailed-deer/; • http://animaldiversity.ummz.umich.edu/accounts/Odocoileus_virginianus/; • http://dnr.wi.gov/org/caer/ce/eek/critter/mammal/fawn.htm; • http://www.fcps.edu/islandcreekes/ecology/white-tailed_deer.htm; • http://www.nhptv.org/natureworks/whitetaileddeer.htm; • Erichsen-Brown, C. 1979. Medicinal and Other Uses of North American Plants. Dover Publications, NY.; • http://www.allaboutbirds.org/guide/Mallard/lifehistory; • http://www.peabodymemphis.com/peabody-ducks/; • http://www.californiaherps.com/snakes/pages/t.s.infernalis.html; • http://www.naturenorth.com/spring/creature/garter/Fgarter.html; • http://www.anapsid.org/garters2.html; • http://masonlab.

< Sources >

science.oregonstate.edu/red-sided-garter-snakehttp://www.nps.gov/lecl/naturescience/common-camas.htm; • http://animaldiversity.ummz.umich.edu/accounts/Lucanus_elaphus/; • http://www.hiltonpond.org/ThisWeek080601.html; • http://animaldiversity.ummz.umich.edu/site/accounts/information/Branta_canadensis.html; • http://www.highbeam.com/doc/1G1-115694656.html; • http://www.humanesociety.org/animals/geese/tips/canada_geese_urban_areas.html; • http://www.illinoiswildflowers.info/prairie/plantx/oh_spiderwortx.htm; • http://animaldiversity.ummz.umich.edu/site/accounts/information/Branta_canadensis.html; • http://www.highbeam.com/doc/1G1-115694656.html; • http://www.humanesociety.org/animals/geese/tips/canada_geese_urban_areas.html •

Black Cherry

http://forestry.about.com/od/hardwoods/tp/Prunus_serotina.htm; • http://www.carolinanature.com/trees/prse.html; • http://www.webpages.uidaho.edu/range556/appl_behave/projects/toxins-wildlife.htm; • http://www.fs.fed.us/database/feis/plants/tree/pruser/all.html; • http://www.missouribotanicalgarden.org/gardens-gardening/your-garden/plant-finder/plant-details/kc/a914/prunus-serotina.aspx; • http://www.wildflower.org/plants/result.php? Id plant=PRSE2; • http://nathanrupley.files.wordpress.com/2011/02/101.jpg; • Read more: http://www.livestrong.com/article/487968-black-cherry-benefits-uric-acid/#ixzz2VSqhiELR; • .http://www.texasbeyondhistory.net/ethnobot/images/black-cherry.html; • http://www.mdidea.com/products/new/new09608.html; • http://www.horseracinghistory.co.uk/hrho/action/viewDocument? Id=1174; • http://www.wschsgrf.org/farm-walking-tour/13; • http://www.mythencyclopedia.com/Fi-Go/Fruit-in-Mythology.html#b#ixzz2VarMwdZN; • www.cherrymkt.org; • http://www.foodreference.com/html/artcherrieshistory.html •

Cherry companions

http://www.birdsource.org/ibs/IBSspecies/cedwax/index.html; • http://www.allaboutbirds.org/guide/cedar_waxwing/lifehistory; • http://www.nhptv.org/natureworks/cedarwaxwing.htm; • http://birding.about.com/od/birdprofiles/p/procedarwax.htm; • http://www.oldandinteresting.com/rushlights.aspx; • http://www.everwilde.com/store/Juncus-interior-Seed.html; • http://www.cmnh.org/site/ResearchandCollections/VertebrateZoology/Research/Treefrogs/GreyTreefrogs.aspx; • http://people.wcsu.edu/pinout/herpetology/hversicolor/nathist.htm; • http://www.ontarionature.org/protect/species/reptiles_and_amphibians/gray_treefrog.php; • http://botit.botany.wisc.edu/toms_fungi/jul2008.html; • http://www.rogersmushrooms.com/gallery/DisplayBlock~bid~5728.asp; • http://imnh.isu.edu/digitalatlas/bio/mammal/Rod/Beaver/beaver.htm; • http://www.arkive.org/american-beaver/castor-canadensis/; • http://animals.about.com/od/rodents/p/beaver.htm; • http://www.theanimalspot.com/americanbeaver.htm; • http://www.nsrl.ttu.edu/tmot1/castcana.htm; • http://www.nhptv.org/natureworks/beaver.htm; • http://users.rcn.com/jkimball.ma.ultranet/BiologyPages/S/Succession.html; • http://www.experience-essential-oils.com/balsam-fir-oil.html; • http://www.localharvest.org/balsam-fir-oil-C23145; • http://www.thefreedictionary.com/Canada+balsam; • http://edis.ifas.ufl.edu/in369; • http://animaldiversity.ummz.umich.edu/accounts/Reticulitermes_flavipes/; • http://www.jgi.doe.gov/whoweare/bioenergy/bioenergy_4.html; • http://www.rook.org/earl/bwca/nature/aquatics/eriocaulon.html; • http://www.ct-botanical-society.org/galleries/eriocaulonaqua.html; • http://amrutaayurved.com/ayurvedicmedicinalplants/plants/choota/; • http://animaldiversity.ummz.umich.edu/accounts/Nymphalis_antiopa/; • http://www.fcps.edu/islandcreekes/ecology/mourning_cloak.htm; • http://www.fcps.edu/islandcreekes/ecology/yellow_pond_lily.htm; • http://www.eattheweeds.com/yellow-pond-lilly-raising-a-wokas/ •

CHAPTER FOUR – LOWER MIDWEST

http://www.nps.gov/miss/riverfacts.htm; • © Dean Klinkenberg, 2011, 2012 http://mississippivalleytraveler.com/river-geology/; • http://fwp.mt.gov/mtoutdoors/HTML/articles/2005/

< Secret Voices from the Forest - Volume II >

< 174 >

MissouriSource.htm; • Gibbon, Guy E.; • Ames, Kenneth M. (eds.). Archaeology of Prehistoric Native America: an encyclopedia. Routledge. ISBN 978-0-8153-0725-9; • http://www.ohiohistorycentral.org/w/ Hopewell_Culture? rec=1283; • http://www.sacredland.org/mississippi-mounds/#sthash.cnHVEc3L. dpuf; • http://www.sacredland.org/mississippi-mounds/; • http://www.memphis.edu/ceri/ compendium/enigma.pdf; • http://www.igsb.uiowa.edu/Browse/rift/mrs.htm •

Pecan

http://forestry.about.com/od/hardwoods/tp/Prunus_serotina.htm; • http://www.carolinanature. com/trees/prse.html; • http://www.webpages.uidaho.edu/range556/appl_behave/projects/toxins-wildlife.htm; • http://www.fs.fed.us/database/feis/plants/tree/pruser/all.html; • http://www. missouribotanicalgarden.org/gardens-gardening/your-garden/plant-finder/plant-details/kc/a914/ prunus-serotina.aspx; • http://www.wildflower.org/plants/result.php? Id plant=PRSE2; • http:// nathanrupley.files.wordpress.com/2011/02/101.jpg; • Read more: http://www.livestrong.com/ article/487968-black-cherry-benefits-uric-acid/#ixzz2VSqhiELR; • .http://www.texasbeyondhistory. net/ethnobot/images/black-cherry.html; • http://www.mdidea.com/products/new/new09608. html; • http://www.horseracinghistory.co.uk/hrho/action/viewDocument? Id=1174; • http:// www.wschsgrf.org/farm-walking-tour/13; • http://www.mythencyclopedia.com/Fi-Go/Fruit-in-Mythology.html#b#ixzz2VarMwdZN; • www.cherrymkt.org; • http://www.foodreference.com/html/ artcherrieshistory.html •

Pecan companions

http://animals.nationalgeographic.com/animals/mammals/armadillo/; • http://www.nsrl.ttu.edu/ tmot1/dasynove.htm; • http://www.nhptv.org/natureworks/armadillo.htm; • http://www.loc.gov/ rr/scitech/mysteries/armadillo.html; • http://www.nwf.org/Wildlife/Wildlife-Library/Mammals/ Nine-Banded-Armadillo.aspx; • http://flowers.about.com/od/Perennial-Flowers/p/Indian-Pink-A-Wildflower-For-The-Hummingbird-Garden.htm; • lhttp://www.anandaapothecary.com/fes-north-american-flower-essences/indian-pink-flower-essence.html; • http://www.natureatcloserange. com/2008/09/indian-pink.html; • http://www.allaboutbirds.org/guide/Lesser_Prairie-Chicken/ lifehistory; • http://www.nrcs.usda.gov/wps/portal/nrcs/n/?ss=16&navid=100120310000000&pnavi d=100120000000000&position=SUBNAVIGATION&ttype=main&navtype=SUBNAVIGATION&pname =Environmental%20Quality%20Incentives%20Program;• http://www.illinoiswildflowers.info/prairie/ plantx/cl_cherryx.htm; • http://www.illinoiswildflowers.info/prairie/plantx/cl_cherryx.htm; • http:// www.crystalyouth.co.za/Documents/Nightshade%20Vegetables%20and%20Arthritis.htm;http://www. naturalmedicinalherbs.net/herbs/p/physalis-heterophylla=clammy-ground-cherry.php; • http://dnr. maryland.gov/mydnr/CreatureFeature/devilcrayfish.asp.; • http://www.dnr.state.md.us/wildlife/ Plants_Wildlife/Devil_Crayfish.asp; • http://cherokeeregistry.com/black_drink.pdf; • Hudson, Charles M., Black Drink: A Native American Tea. University of Georgia Press, 1979; • http://www.allaboutbirds. org/guide/Wood_Duck/lifehistory; • http://www.mushroomexpert.com/phallaceae.html; • http:// solutionsforyourlife.ufl.edu/hot_topics/lawn_and_garden/stinkhorns.html; • http://www.tpwd. state.tx.us/huntwild/wild/species/bronzefrog/http://www.fs.fed.us/wildflowers/plant-of-the-week/ipomopsis_aggregata.shtml; • http://eco.cellsignal.com/04/scarlet.html; • http://www.life. illinois.edu/paige/overcomp.html; • M. J. Sheehan & E. A. Tibbetts (2011). Specialized Face Learning Is Associated with Individual Recognition in Paper Wasps. Science. 334. 1272-1275.; http://www.dailymail. co.uk/debate/article-2406094/ •

Catalpa

http://forestry.about.com/od/alternativeforest/ss/catalpa_7.htm; • httpwww.lovelycitizen.com/ entry/47801/; • http://www.illinoiswildflowers.info/trees/plants/n_catalpa.html; • http:// forumhome.org/big-tree-for-june-northern-catalpa-catalpa-speciosa-p11418-105.htm; • http://warnell. forestry.uga.edu/service/library/index.php3?doc ID=178&docHistory%5B%5D=2; • http://www.

< 175 >

< Sources >

ag.auburn.edu/enpl/bulletins/catalpasphinx/catalpasphinx; • http://warnell.forestry.uga.edu/ service/library/index.php3?docID=178&docHistory%5B%5D=2; • Lewis, M.J.T., "Railways in the Greek and Roman World," in Guy, A. / Rees, J. (eds), *Early Railways. A Selection of Papers from the First International Early Railways Conference* (2001), pp. 8–19 (11); • http://tigger.uic.edu/~rjensen/railroad. htm •

Catalpa companions

http://animaldiversity.ummz.umich.edu/accounts/Vulpes_vulpes/; • http://www.dailymail. co.uk/news/article-1343802/; • http://www.gpnc.org/osage.htm; • http://old.post-gazette.com/ magazine/20000902monkeyballs6.asp; • https://ohiodnr.com/forestry/trees/osage_orange/ tabid/5403/Default.aspx; • http://www.burkemuseum.org/spidermyth/myths/skineggs.html; • http://hedgeapple.com; • http://www.ag.auburn.edu/enpl/bulletins/catalpasphinx/catalpasphinx. htm; • https://insects.tamu.edu/fieldguide/cimg305.html; • http://www.sisterzeus.com/BlueCoh. htm; • http://www.mountainroseherbs.com/learn/blue_cohosh.php; • http://www.healthy.net/ scr/MMedica.aspx?Id=165; • http://www.chelydra.org/common_alligator_snapping_turtle.html; • http://nationalzoo.si.edu/Animals/ReptilesAmphibians/Facts/FactSheets/Alligatorsnappingturtle. cfm; • http://animals.nationalgeographic.com/animals/reptiles/alligator-snapping-turtle/; • http:// www.naturalnews.com/036237_bee_balm_healing_cooking.html; • http://www.gardensablaze. com/HerbBeeBalmMed.htm; • http://www.nhptv.org/natureworks/americanbadger.htm; • http:// animaldiversity.ummz.umich.edu/accounts/Taxidea_taxus/; • http://www.theanimalspot.com/ americanbadger.htm; • http://www.proflowers.com/guide/texas-state-flower-the-bluebonnet; • http:// www.library.illinois.edu/vex/toxic/lupine/lupine.htm; • http://www.hort.purdue.edu/newcrop/ afcm/lupine.html; • http://www.allaboutbirds.org/guide/American_Robin/lifehistory; • http:// animaldiversity.ummz.umich.edu/accounts/Turdus_migratorius/; • http://www.illinoiswildflowers. info/prairie/plantx/hry_puccoonx.htm; • http://www.allaboutbirds.org/guide/Barn_Owl/lifehistory; • http://floranorthamerica.org •

Common Persimmon

http://faculty.salisbury.edu/~chbriand/PDFs/Huntia05.pdf; • Brand, C.H., The Common Persimmon (Diospyros virginian a L.): The history of an underutilized fruit tree (16th – 19th centuries. 2005. Hunt Institute for Botanical Documentation. Chisholm, Hugh, ed. (1911). "Persimmon". Encyclopædia Britannica (11th ed.). Cambridge University Press; • http://www.na.fs.fed.us/spfo/pubs/silvics_ manual/volume_2/diospyros/virginiana.htm; • http://www.missouribotanicalgarden.org/gardens- gardening/your-garden/plant-finder/plant-details/kc/h740/diospyros-virginiana.aspx; • http://www. fs.fed.us/database/feis/plants/tree/diovir/all.html; • http://www.reference.com/browse/persimmon; • http://www.wildflower.org/plants/result.php? Id plant=DIVI5; • http://www.ncausa.org/i4a/ pages/index.cfm?pageid=68 •

Persimmon companions

http://www.allaboutbirds.org/guide/Bald_Eagle/lifehistory; • http://www.baldeagleinfo.com; • http://www.chieftain.com/outdoors/the-most-majestic-of-all-bald-eagles-plentiful-as-impressive/ article_a1735b46-699c-11e2-8d1a-0019bb2963f4.html; • http://botit.botany.wisc.edu/toms_fungi/ march97.html; • http://www.mushroomexpert.com/flammulina_velutipes.html; • http:// wiseacre-gardens.com/wordpress/velvet-foot-mushroom/ ; • http://www-museum.unl.edu/ research/entomology/endanger.htm.; • http://www.rwpzoo.org/143/american-burying-beetle- repopulation-project; • http://www.fws.gov/southdakotafieldoffice/BEETLE.HTM; • http:// www.dec.ny.gov/animals/7124.html; • http://www.stlzoo.org/conservation/wildcare-institute/ americanburyingbeetleconse/; • http://www.adirondackvic.org/Adirondack-Wildflowers-Spotted- Touch-Me-Not-Impatiens-capensis.html; • http://mdc.mo.gov/discover-nature/field-guide/spotted- touch-me-not-jewelweed; • http://www.fcps.edu/islandcreekes/ecology/luna_moth.htm; • http://

animaldiversity.ummz.umich.edu/accounts/Actias_luna/; • http://www.psu.edu/dept/nkbiology/
naturetrail/speciespages/jackinpulpit.htm; • http://www.eattheweeds.com/arisaema-triphyllum-jack-
and-jill-and-no-hill-2/; • http://www.radfordpl.org/wildwood/today/species_of_the_week/SOW39_
Jack_in_the_Pulpit.htm; • http://animals.nationalgeographic.com/animals/mammals/raccoon/; •
http://www.fcps.edu/islandcreekes/ecology/raccoon.htm; • http://www.nhptv.org/natureworks/
raccoon.htm; • http://animaldiversity.ummz.umich.edu/accounts/Procyon_lotor/; • http://www.
fs.fed.us/wildflowers/plant-of-the-week/triphora_trianthophora.shtml; • http://floraofohio.blogspot.
com/2011/08/tale-of-three-birds.html; • http://jimmccormac.blogspot.com/search/label/three-
birds%20orchid; • http://www.fws.gov/midwest/endangered/amphibians/ozhe/ •

ABOUT THE AUTHOR

Laura Merrill makes her home off-grid on a high mesa outside Taos, New Mexico. Her companions are several cats and a variety of wildlife including, but not limited to, coyote, pronghorn antelope, elk, endless bunnies and jackrabbits, ravens, mountain bluebirds, rattlesnakes, and tarantulas. The cats stay in, and everything else stays out.

During her association with a small spiritual community, Laura was encouraged to develop her natural ability to receive mental impressions — not only from other people, but from plants and animals as well.

Over the subsequent forty years, she has refined this capacity into a process by which she can communicate with the trees. No attempt is made to convince anyone that a tree has a consciousness that can be contacted — you may believe it or not, as Ripley would say.

Please visit www.laurajmerrilltreetalker.com for additional information.

About the Poet

Brian Mitchell has composed featured poems for each tree and the opening haiku for the chapters, using information Laura gathered from her communication with them. He and Laura became friends in 1971 through their mutual association with the aforementioned community. After thirty-five years of separately following their own pursuits, the two reconnected via the Internet, and have remained in contact ever since.

Brian spent several years in the U.S., living and working in New Orleans, Chicago, and St. Louis, Missouri, where he earned his Master's Degree in Creative Writing from Washington University. He is now retired and owns a rural freehold in Wales, where he writes, renovates, and has planted his own personal forest of over a thousand trees.

Please visit www.brianmitchellworks.net for additional information.